SECRET S...

of

BLETCHLE...

Psychological Warfare

John A. Ta...

John A. ...

1
9
9
15
15
35
35
47
47
61
61
73
73
89
89
107
107
113
113
131
131
141
141
147
147

"Come, come, gentlemen, a domestic animal, three letters, and it begins with C."

ACKNOWLEDGEMENTS

Bletchley Park and the codebreaking achievements of World War Two are now well known across the world. Yet within the immediate district many other Secret Intelligence activities were also being carried on, and of those involving propaganda, the prime source of reference are the books 'Black Boomerang' and 'The Black Game', respectively by Sefton Delmer and Ellic Howe. Both men wrote from first hand experience, and for the general story of propaganda, their information is gratefully acknowledged as having been invaluable.

As for details concerning the more local aspects, kind acknowledgement is made as follows:

Mr. Ingram Murray for invaluable source material, personal knowledge and assistance with the final editing.

Mr. P. Luck, Mr. R. Tink, Mrs. R. Mottram, Mr. S. Halliday, Mr. W. Dunkley, Mr. D. White, Mr. G. Pidgeon, Mr. I. Pennington, for their extensive contributions of information, reminiscence and illustrations.

The Duke of Bedford, for kindly agreeing to perform the unveiling of a commemorative plaque at the wartime broadcast studio of Milton Bryan.

Mr. Brian Cairns, Marylands College.

David and Debra Rixon for accepting the challenge to produce an associated video, available from Grindelwald Productions, P.O. Box 38, Princes Risborough, Bucks, HP27 9BG.

Jonathan Marks, the producer of a radio programme on the subject. Neil Rees, for his extensive knowledge of the Czechoslovakian aspects.

Tracy Whitmore, of the Bletchley Community Heritage Initiative, for assistance with the printing and editing of the final draft.

Audrey Wind and John Elgar-Whinney, for proof reading the final text and supplying valued illustrations.

Mrs. Jill Forbes, Headteacher of Emerson Valley School, Milton Keynes, for allowing the initial research for this project to be displayed via a school orientated website, courtesy of the Open University and the Millennium Awards Commission.

Amanda Ainger, for her enthusiasm and continued encouragement.

EMERSON VALLEY SCHOOL Hodder Lane,
Emerson Valley, Milton Keynes MK4 2JR Telephone: 01908
507914 Fax: 01908 507915
e-mailemersonvalley@Milton-Keynes.Gov.UK
Headteacher: Mrs **Jill** Forbes MA(Ed) F. Col. **P.**

19.11.02

When I received information about the CLUTCH Club (Computer Literacy and Understanding Through Community History), I was hopeful that some of the parents of Emerson Valley School Children would be interested in taking part in this project.

I was pleased that a member of staff and a group of parents took up the challenge and produced a web site that the school and they could be proud of. It was an innovative way of developing parent partnership with an outcome to be proud of.

Many hours of hard work were put into researching and collating information for this site.

Not content with producing pages for the website John Taylor has continued his interest in this subject to produce this book.

Jill Forbes

Headteacher of Emerson Valley School

Woburn Abbey

I first met John Taylor at the end of 2000 when he wrote asking me to unveil a plaque on what had been known locally as 'the film studio' at Milton Bryan, a small village just outside the Park wall. Intrigued, I asked to hear more about it and thus began an amazing journey into the daily life and activities of the people
who worked there during the war. On September 4[1] 2002 the plaque, in recognition of those largely unsung workers, was unveiled in a small ceremony at Milton Bryan beautifully orchestrated by Mr Taylor with period cars, uniforms and even a NAAFI tea tent! It was fascinating to meet and talk with people who had been involved with the propaganda unit and listen to their stories first hand.

I do hope that you will enjoy your journey into this small chapter of history and take time to reflect on the work and sacrifice given by others during the war so that we might live as we do today.

Bedford.

The Duke of Bedford
February 2004

ABOUT THE AUTHOR

John Taylor has lived and worked in the district for many years and first became interested in the local history of the region at the beginnings of the New City, when much of the once familiar countryside began to disappear under the new developments, and the previous communities began to lose their individuality.

In 1974 had come the revelation of the wartime codebreaking activities at Bletchley Park, and during his delvings into the more general history of the area, it gradually became apparent, from brief, and often obscure sources, that a whole range of other secret intelligence activities had also been carried out in the immediate region during the wartime years.

Not least was a brief newspaper report in Feb. 1946 revealing that a number of Germans has been caught smuggling clothing and food parcels out of Britain, the food parcels bearing addresses in Aspley Guise. In a curt response, the War Office issued a statement: 'Authority has been given to those German prisoners of war who had obtained civilian clothes for the performance of duties in aid of this country, to retain civilian clothes provided their total baggage was restricted to the normal personal allowance of 112lb for officers and 56lb for other ranks.' This proved hardly illuminating but, deeply involved with the 'black' propaganda organisation based around Woburn Abbey, Sefton Delmer then recorded his role in the book 'Black Boomerang' and, together with a later book by Ellic Howe, this information provided a general backgound for such activities. So began a separate project, to research and write up the local story.

However, there were also many other secret operations being carried out. These had not been fully documented, but by talking to the personnel involved it has become possible to finally reveal this additional story, and thereby afford a long overdue credit to their participation and achievements.

John Taylor has written a number of books about the history of the Bletchley area and surrounding towns and villages. He writes a regular column for the Milton Keynes Citizen. His recent publications include a five volume account of North Bucks during the First World War.

INTRODUCTION

Bletchley Park is now famous for its secret intelligence activities during World War Two, but there was also another secret war being waged from centres within the same district.. Bletchley Park was chosen for the codebreaking headquarters because it was safe from the London Blitz yet still, linked by good road and rail communications, close enough to the London centres of Government. For the same reasons several other secret wartime organisations transferred their operations to this district, and their activities ranged from subversive and sometimes pornographic propaganda to radio communication centres and the training of secret agents. The purpose of this book is to now tell their lesser-known story – 'the other secret war'.

Propaganda, trying to influence enemy opinion with words, was initially the responsibility of Department Electra House, locally based at Woburn Abbey. They produced leaflets and other documents to be dropped from aircraft or infiltrated by secret agents and also began propaganda radio broadcasts. They were recorded onto discs at a secret recording studio, and then taken by Secret Service cars to radio transmitters hidden in the countryside.

Employing Foreign Office staff and assisted by many experts, the Political Intelligence Department at Woburn gauged the conditions within enemy territory. Analysing many sources of intelligence, they operated from country premises on the outskirts of Woburn that had once been a model hospital, founded by the Duchess of Bedford.

In 1940 the Prime Minister, Winston Churchill, set up a special sabotage organisation to operate in enemy territory. This was known as the Special Operations Executive – S.O.E. – and divided into two sections. One, (SO1), dealt with propaganda, absorbing the duties of the previous Department Electra House. The other, (SO2), dealt with active operations and ran not only a local training school for special agents but also radio communication stations. Agents were flown out on their secret missions In black painted aircraft from nearby airfields.

In 1941 Churchill then initiated a new propaganda organisation, to be known as the Political Warfare Executive. From Woburn Abbey this controlled the 'black' side of the broadcast operations, transmitting radio programmes that pretended to be run by dissident groups from within the occupied countries. Using the largest radio transmitter in Europe, from purpose built studios at Milton Bryan they could also take over enemy radio stations and, by mimicking the announcers, hoax the Germans into believing all manner of false information.

A Special Communications Unit sent intelligence decodes from Bletchley Park to Allied Commanders overseas from a hilltop radio centre near Whaddon. Other radio stations maintained contact with secret agents operating undercover in occupied

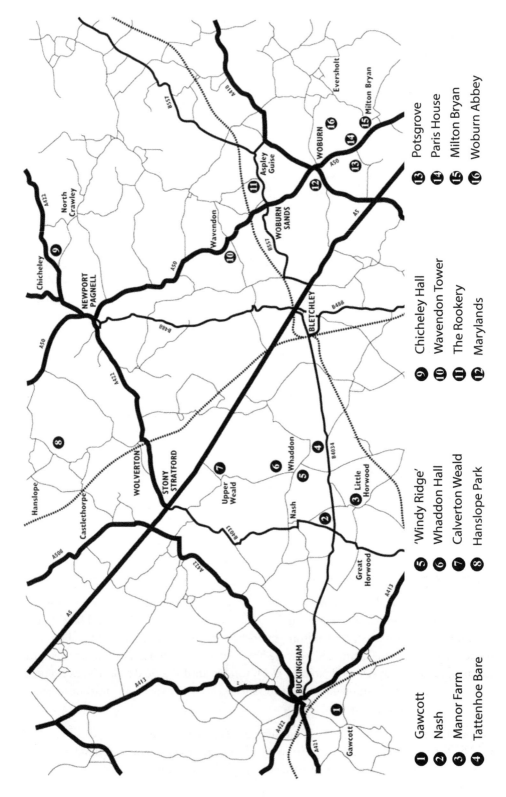

1. Gawcott
2. Nash
3. Manor Farm
4. Tattenhoe Bare
5. 'Windy Ridge'
6. Whaddon Hall
7. Calverton Weald
8. Hanslope Park
9. Chicheley Hall
10. Wavendon Tower
11. The Rookery
12. Marylands
13. Potsgrove
14. Paris House
15. Milton Bryan
16. Woburn Abbey

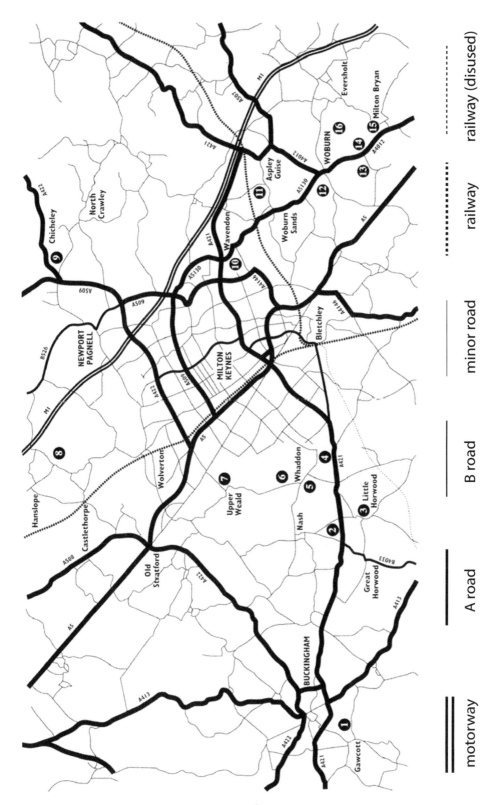

motorway   A road   B road   minor road   railway   railway (disused)

Cables Map

Military or
Government
Departments
OZWH
Whaddon Hall
OZWR
Windy Ridge
OZBR
Whaddon Bare
OBP
Bletchley Park
(Station X)
OZSH
Stoke Hammond
(RAF)
OZWT
Wavendon Tower
OXCH
Chicheley Manor
OWA
Woburn Abbey
OMB
Milton Bryan
OCFM
Hockliffe
(Czech W/T)
ODUN
Dunstable
Meteorological HQ

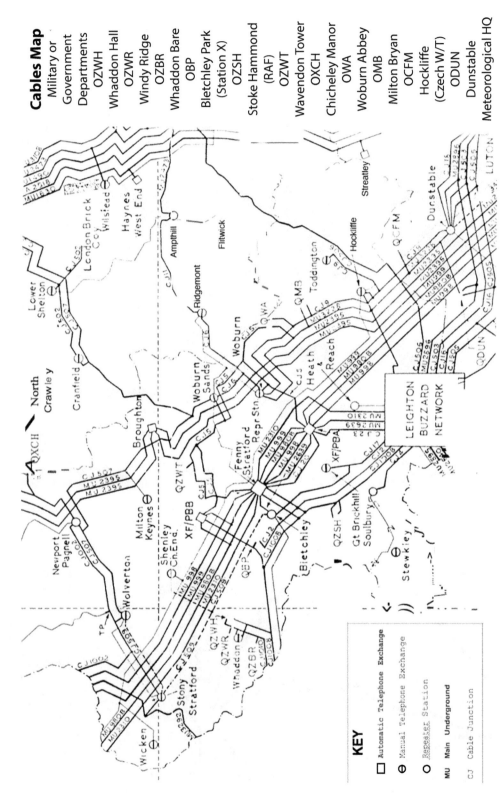

KEY

☐   Automatic Telephone Exchange

⊖   Manual Telephone Exchange

○   Repeater Station

MU   Main Underground

CJ   Cable Junction

4

territory. Hidden near a village farm, secret laboratories and workshops designed and manufactured the covert wireless equipment to be used by these agents.

The Radio Security Service constantly monitored enemy radio transmissions from Hanslope Park. The information was then analysed by the intelligence services and passed on to those agencies best able to use the information.

These then were the other intelligence organisations, operating during World War Two from the district around Bletchley Park, and in the following chapters their more detailed role and achievements will be revealed.

Many of the nation's main communication cables passed along the line of the Watling Street, the signals being amplified at regular distances by a series of 'repeater stations'. The Fenny Stratford repeater station, which has been demolished in recent years, was of great importance during World War Two. Cables were laid from here to link the surrounding secret intelligence sites with the national network, which was especially necessary to communicate with the centres of Government in London.

THE FENNY STRATFORD REPEATER STATION

Before the 1920s, telephone wires were often carried along many of the nation's main highways by wooden poles. This overhead arrangement was used as a means to limit the loss of signal between the very large distances that were spanned. A small 'test and intercept' hut, built of brick, was constructed for the Post Office engineering department at Fenny Stratford, near the canal bridge, to test the lines that passed along the Watling Street, in the early part of the century. It was under the charge of Mr. F. Young and Mr. G. Line. As the amount of telecommunications traffic increased, it then became impractical to continue with the above ground system due to the size and cost. Instead, cables were increasingly laid underground, but because these cables had a smaller diameter, the signal loss increased and it became necessary to introduce 'repeater stations', typically spaced 45 miles apart, to amplify the signal.

In 1923, whereupon, 'Fenny Stratford will become once again an important telegraphic and telephonic centre', it was therefore proposed to build a 'telephone relay station' on the same site as the brick hut, and, completed in 1924, the Fenny Stratford repeater station comprised two storeys with a reinforced concrete floor, and was amongst the first in the country. The sections were transported from Bletchley station on four horse drays, initially two Ruston and Hornsby heavy oil engines. These engines descended from the type pioneered by the Fenny Stratford engineer Akroyd Stuart, and generated the electricity.

With the completion of the repeater station, the telephone linemen then moved to George Street and after a few years transferred to Bletchley Park. One of the personnel at the repeater station was a Boer War veteran, Alfred Peerless, who in 1896, as a member of the Telegraph Battalion of the Royal Engineers, had assisted in the early wireless experiments conducted by Marconi on Salisbury Plain. With the aerials held aloft by kites and balloons, his job was to maintain liaison between the transmitter and receiver by means of flag signals. Many of the main national cables passed through the Fenny Stratford repeater station, and swift measures to safeguard the building were taken at the outbreak of World War Two, including the provision of heavy steel shutters on the inside of those windows facing the Watling Street, and the building of small bunkers either side of the entrance. Such measures were indeed imperative, since many new circuits would be laid to serve the several nearby wartime secret establishments, including Bletchley Park, to which a cable was laid in 1938. As seen on the map, in case the Fenny Stratford repeater station was damaged by enemy action, along the Watling Street two additional repeater stations were situated, one north and one south, from where, if necessary, a redirection of cable traffic could be made. After the war, in 1949, following many years of use one of the heavy oil engines sustained a cracked cylinder head and was used to provide spares for the other engine until purchased by the original manufacturers in August 1966. A new 3 cylinder engine was then installed as an auxiliary power supply.

With the advance of technology, the need for repeater stations declined and the example at Fenny Stratford was officially closed on October 9th 1979. The following year much of the equipment was then removed, some being sent to museums, and after use for several years as storage, the building was then demolished.

THE CZECH WIRELESS STATION AT HOCKLIFFE

The importance of observing security procedures

On July 3rd 1940 Edvard Benes had been recognised as the head of the provincial Czech Government exiled in Britain, and in August Robert Bruce Lockhart, of the Political Intelligence Department, was appointed by the Foreign Office as the British Representative. Initially Benes had been allocated a villa in Gwendolen Avenue, London but with the increasing danger from German air raids, Lockhart arranged accommodation for him in the village of Aston Abbotts, near Wing as a safer refuge. Later, this would also prove more convenient for maintaining contact with the Czech wireless station at Hockliffe, through which Benes could communicate with the overseas radio stations of Czech Intelligence, military missions and the Czech Resistance in the German controlled Protectorate of Bohemia and Moravia.

Some of the families of the Czech intelligence officers lived at Addington manor house, near Winslow, and initially, in September 1939, the Czech Military Radio Centre, the V.R.U., had begun working from Rosendale Road, West Dulwich. When this was bombed, radio contact with the Czech resistance was maintained from a communications station at Woldingham, and then Hockliffe, where the facilities had been provided by the Special Operations Executive. As will be seen from the cable map, the station was linked into the national network of trunk cables, and this enabled direct communication with the Czech centres of importance as well as local secret intelligence organisations and the centres of Government in London.

British Intelligence monitored the activities of the station but, as apparent from this archive letter, concerns sometimes arose.

6

CZECH WIRELESS STATION (Hockliffe)

Major   visited the station yesterday and was given a thorough look-
round by the personnel there. The station appeared to be now working smoothly
and happily, but he elicited one remarkable fact which I wish to bring to your
notice for urgent action.

2.   Despite repeated warnings from us (including a personal one from C.S.S.
to MORAVEC,) they are communicating regularly with the PARIS station which, as
we all know, is run by the Germans. Major   informs me that the
following messages have been passed recently:-

        November: 3 messages received: 9 sent.
        December: 8 messages received: 8 sent.

3.   This state of affairs seems to me (unless I misread the situation)
highly undesirable for the following reasons:-

     (a) From a security point of view: we do not wish the Germans &
     the Czechs to be in contact with each other by means of codes over
which we have no control.

     (b) This procedure has presumably effectively blown the Czechs' new
main station and therefore will prejudice future communications
with the Protectorate.

     (c) From an Intelligence point of view, the Czechs have refused to
take C.S.S's warnings in earnest and they are now receiving
tendentious reports from the Germans.

     We know that 'planted' information has recently been passed by
BENES through BRUCE LOCKHART to the Foreign Office, and I should
not be surprised to learn that it is coming in by this method.

4.   I will bring this matter to the notice of C.S.S., but before doing so,
I would like to have your reactions as it is obviously in the first place a
question of wireless security.   I shall be interested to hear Major TILL's
views on the present state of affairs.

C.P.O.
25.12.42

THE DAY WAR BROKE OUT

"As a member of a territorial anti-aircraft battery from South London (Streatham, in fact - unkindly referred to as the "plus fours but no breakfast" area) we had been deployed to our war stations. In my case to our No. 3 Troop HQ site on the Duke of Bedford's estate between the villages of Milton Brian and Eversholt. Very quiet but, being under canvas, not happy with the incessant rain. At 9.10 a.m. on the day in question we were ordered to action stations and remained so until given the stand down at 1.15 p.m. The only sign of any activity was a solitary Avro Anson plane passing over the site at about 11.00 a.m. A sigh of relief - the site and the gun pit being flooded! Our food was being cooked out in the open by our worthy but unscrupulous cook who had worked as a gravedigger! I wonder if the Duke's gamekeeper, if he's still alive, remembers complaining to my Troop Officer, alleg¬ing the disappearance of some of his pheasants from the area to the rear of our cook's stove?!! What followed for the rest of the war is another story - of book length.

Lance Bombardier (Acting Unpaid)"

The Day War Broke Out *Focus Magazine*

CHAPTER ONE

THE POLITICAL INTELLIGENCE DEPARTMENT

The role of the Political Intelligence Department was to gather information on behalf of the Foreign Office concerning contemporary conditions within various European countries. Originally formed during the First World War, as the Second World War became inevitable the Department had been reactivated for a similar task, but the speed of the German advance and the rapid collapse of many European countries tended to extinguish the political purpose. With the declining need for P.I.D., organisations for sabotage and subversion then assumed priority.

Born in Australia, the son of a distinguished Greek scholar, Reginald 'Rex' Leeper had secured a permanent position at the Foreign Office in 1920 and before World War Two became head of the Foreign Office News Department.

As war became inevitable in the wake of the Munich Crisis, in 1938 he then began to revive and reorganise an overt branch of the Foreign Office, the Political Intelligence Department, which had been active during the First World War. The purpose of the Department was to glean information concerning European countries and compile reports, and as the head Reginald Leeper also held the position of Foreign Office advisor to the Department of Propaganda in Enemy Countries (Department Electra House) at Woburn Abbey. This dictated a need for the headquarters of P.I.D. to be within the same district, and to staff the organisation he secured the service of various experts.

Referred to vaguely as being 'in the country', for reasons of security their initial accommodation was a fairly insubstantial red brick 'villa', situated on the Woburn Abbey estate, adjacent to the gates of Woburn Park. Codenamed 'Foxgrove', this had once been the home of Lady Ampthill but now had to suffice as both the living and working conditions for the P.I.D. team. This included an Oxford historian, E. Woodward, the German expert, Chris Warner of the Foreign Office, who deputised for Leeper in his absence, and an Italian expert, who had written an authoritative book on the Mediterranean, Lieutenant Commander George Martelli, who had served in the Navy during World War One. He eventually became involved in the Italian Region of the later mentioned S01. Of perhaps greater significance, in view of his future role in the propaganda activities, also recruited was Robert Bruce Lockhart, who had first made Leeper's acquaintance in 1917, having in 1912 been posted to Moscow as Vice Consul. He was later appointed as Acting Consul General but was soon ordered back on the pretence of 'sick leave', actually a cover for an alleged scandal! Returning to Russia after the Revolution, he then became involved in covert activities. As for the local region, he claimed an ancestral association through a collateral forebear, James Boswell, the biographer of Dr. Johnson, and, due to family connections with Crawley Grange, in North Crawley church may be seen several memorials, including an ovoid tablet of note.

Froxfield Lodge

Situated near to one of the entrance gates of Woburn Park, Froxfield Lodge became the initial home for members of the Political Intelligence Department. Codenamed 'Foxgrove', the house proved too small for efficient working but nevertheless, a few months later, was the venue for a meeting of the estate workers, called together to be told that because of the war they could not be given a payrise! (J. Taylor)

Though originally intended for the Russian section, when the original candidate for Central Europe and the Balkans became ineligible Lockhart filled this position, excepting Germany and Austria. Reporting for duty on September 10th, 1939, he took the afternoon train to Dunstable where Leeper met him by car. They then drove to the P.I.D. headquarters, where Lockhart was assigned an attic bedroom which also served as his study. However, these cramped conditions proved hardly suitable for his demanding role and within a week the P.I.D. personnel were transferred from 'Foxgrove' to the more commodious 'Marylands', just outside the village of Woburn. Yet even so, although 'not bad as a building, for it is well lighted and well situated', this still remained far from ideal. 'We will be an awful scrum, and there will be about six wives, daughters, etc … Unless I can get a writing table for my bedroom I shall go mad'. Indeed, this seemed a not unreasonable request, for, as well as being tasked with preparing special memorandums for the Foreign Office, each week he also had to write a review regarding his allotted countries, which then contributed to a 'Political Summary', intended to provide guidance for other departments.

For his weekly intelligence summary, Lockhart produced a report of about 2000 words, subsequently despatched to the relevant political departments of the Foreign Office for final approval. In order to cope with this workload, each morning Lockhart arose early, made his own tea and completed much of the writing before breakfast. The remainder of the day would mostly be taken up with meetings and planning. Having so many countries to administer, with the associated need to liaise with his many contacts, he found it more convenient to take a room at his London club, and so spent half the week in the Capital and the other half at Marylands. A very 'political animal', needing to keep in touch with his patrons, especially Anthony Eden, the Foreign Secretary, this also resolved that requirement as well.

Having met with his Balkan contacts, during these visits he would then call for a routine exchange of information at the Foreign Office where the Under Secretaries of the two departments controlling his work, the Southern and the Central, were respectively Sir Orme Sargent and William Strang. Perhaps understandably, neither greatly approved of a Foreign Office department being situated in the remote depths of Bedfordshire and so, in line with the sentiments of the actual staff, moves were soon put in hand for a relocation back to London. Accordingly, on August 19th, 1940, Lockhart duly compiled his last summary at Marylands and prepared to leave on the Thursday, the same day as the heavy baggage. The rest of the staff would follow the next day.

Their new office was located in Lansdowne House, Fitzmaurice Place, W1, where some of the staff – Reginald Leeper, Valentine Williams and Dallas Brooks – would at least enjoy the welcome benefit of armchairs! Yet, as head of the department, Reginald Leeper still harboured doubts about the move, even to the extent of seeking a return to 'the country', which he deemed more appropriate 'for thinking'. However, London remained as the centre of operations, and as part of their output P.I.D. produced a regular 'Propaganda Nuggets', concentrating mostly on those forecasts and assertions

Marylands

In the early days of the war, Marylands soon became a more spacious accommodation for the Political Intelligence Department team, before housing the printing facilities for the propaganda organisation. Designed to accommodate a dozen or so patients from Woburn and the immediate district, it had been originally founded as a cottage hospital by Mary, Duchess of Bedford, wife of the 11th Duke, in 1903. The premises were until recently in use as a college for adult education. (Mr. B. Cairns)

made by the Nazis which had not yet been fulfilled.

On the recommendation of Reginald Leeper, apart from his P.I.D. duties in August 1940 Robert Bruce Lockhart accepted an invitation to fulfill the Foreign Office position of British Representative to Edvard Beneš and the exiled Czechoslovak Government in Britain. Beneš had been recognised by the British as the head of the provincial Czechoslovak Government on July 3rd 1940, with accommodation arranged through a nephew of Benes at a villa in Gwendolen Avenue, London. With the onset of bombing, Lockhart then helped to obtain a house for him at Aston Abbotts, near Wing, which had once been the home of the Polar explorer, Sir John Ross, and indeed this proved a fortunate move, for the shelter in the London villa would receive a direct hit. A platoon of the Czechoslovak army was also based in Aston Abbotts, several Cabinet ministers lived in nearby Wingrave, and Addington House, near Winslow, provided accommodation for several families of Czechoslovak Intelligence officers. As for Lockhart, when his small flat in Duke of York Street was bombed out, he moved to the East India and Sports Club.

The Czechoslovak Secret Intelligence had spies in the German Army who, before information became available from Enigma, were a main source of intelligence to the British regarding German army movements. In England, the Czech Military Radio Centre (Vojenska Radiova Ustredna, or V.R.U.) employed several excellent radio operators who were supplemented by members of the 1st Czechoslovak Independent Brigade's Signals Company, and in September 1939 the organisation began working from 41 Rosendale Road, West Dulwich, one of three villas rented for the intelligence section. Summoned from France, Lieutenant Jaroslav Stuchly became the first commander of the V.R.U. in England and when Dulwich was bombed, radio contact with the Czech Resistance was maintained from a communications station at Woldingham, and then Hockliffe, situated on the elevation of a field on College Farm, (now Trinity Hall Farm), with huts provided near a hedge as accommodation for the personnel.

The facilities for the Czechoslovakian Intelligence Service had been built by S.O.E., and from Hockcliffe they could communicate with the overseas radio stations of Czech Intelligence, military missions, and the Czech Resistance in the German controlled Protectorate of Bohemia and Moravia, (now the Czech Republic). The Czechoslovak military also worked with S.O.E. in the training of Army volunteers from Leamington Spa, where the Army was based, and following their instruction at Chicheley Hall, the Czechoslovak agents were flown out from Tempsford airfield and parachuted into Czechoslovakia. Constant communications had been maintained with General Elias, the Czech Prime Minister under the Germans, until, on Reinhard Heydrich becoming the German Governor of Bohemia and Moravia, Elias was taken to Berlin and condemned to death. In fact, one of the clandestine missions was to assassinate Heydrich.

As for the Political Intelligence Department, facing a declining need in March 1942, at Leeper's suggestion a decision was made to abolish the position of B.B.C. Liaison Officer, and in April of the following year the Department itself was disbanded.

Many of the staff found alternative employment at a new Foreign Office Research Department at Balliol College, Oxford, which thereon assumed the task of producing the weekly intelligence summaries. Nevertheless, if only in name, P.I.D. lived on, the title being taken in 1941 as cover for the newly created Political Warfare Executive. Further information on the role of P.I.D. may currently be found in documents held at the Public Record Office and also the Hoover Library.

College Farm

College Farm, (now Trinity Hall Farm), near Hockliffe, was the situation for a Czech secret radio station, the facilities for which were provided by the British Special Operations Executive. In the photograph, towards the left may be seen two Nissen huts, (now demolished), that housed the personnel. The actual radio station was located on the rise of a field, just off the upper edge of the photograph. At the turn of the nineteenth century the novelist Arnold Bennett rented the farm and there wrote one of his less well-known works 'Teresa of Watling Street'. During World War One, he was then recruited by the Department of Propaganda in Enemy Countries. The premises were situated at Crewe House, Curzon Street, London, and had been obtained by Campbell Stuart, who would play an important and local role in the reactivated propaganda organisation during World War Two.

Lord Halifax

By the advice of Lord Halifax, during the 1930s the Foreign Office began plans to establish 'non overt' means of propaganda. As Lord Irwin, he had been Viceroy of India from 1926 until 1931 and in February 1938 succeeded Anthony Eden as Foreign Secretary. (War Illustrated)

Sir Campbell Stuart

Born in Montreal in 1885, Campbell Stuart was descended from William Smith of Newport Pagnell, Buckinghamshire, whose son, Thomas, had married Miss Odell, from a wealthy Buckinghamshire family. The couple then emigrated to New York in 1915.

As a Major, during World War One Campbell Stuart had the ambition to compose his Irish Canadian regiment of half Protestants and half Catholics, and these endeavours attracted the approving attention of the newspaper proprietor Lord Northcliffe. When Northcliffe was made Director of Propaganda in Enemy Countries, Campbell Stuart became his deputy and after World War One was awarded a knighthood for his achievements. Thus, with the prospect of another World War, Campbell Stuart became the natural choice to undertake similar duties.

(M. Guynor)

CHAPTER TWO

DEPARTMENT ELECTRA HOUSE

As war became inevitable, the Government began organising the means to employ propaganda as an offensive measure. From his experience in a similar role during World War One, Sir Campbell Stuart was appointed to head such an organisation, which became known as Department Electra House. From Woburn Abbey and associated centres nearby, during a fairly brief existence the foundations of both printed and broadcast propaganda were then laid. These were duly developed by a branch of the Special Operations Executive, when Electra House was absorbed into that organisation in July 1940.

In view of the German rearmament, apart from the overt Ministry of Information during the 1930s, plans had been made by the Foreign Office, under the advice of Lord Halifax, to establish a small section for investigating other means of propaganda. Aside from publications – primarily newspapers – a main source of information, regarding conditions inside Germany, came meanwhile from refugees escaping Nazi persecution, but as the international crisis deepened and the potential for such intelligence lessened, the government pursued a more sophisticated approach.

During World War One Colin Campbell Stuart, a Canadian, had been involved with the successful propaganda activities of Crewe House, the headquarters that he secured in Curzon Street, London, for Lord Northcliffe, then Director of Propaganda in Enemy Countries. In view of this experience, for which he was awarded a knighthood, following a meeting with the head of the Secret Service, 'C', (Admiral Sinclair) he was therefore asked by Sir Warren Fisher, head of the Civil Service, to begin recruiting the necessary staff for a similar department.

As chief staff officer, after liaising with the various military intelligence departments, he selected Lt. Col. Reginald Alexander Dallas Brooks, an Australian who had served with distinction in the Royal Marines during World War One, being awarded both the DSO and the Croix de Guerre. Sir Campbell Stuart had first made his acquaintance in South Africa and the appointment owed much to the assistance of Sir Campbell Stuart's friend, Sir Roger Backhouse, the First Sea Lord. R.J. Shaw, a former member of *Times*, of which Sir Campbell Stuart had once been a director, became head of the section and Valentine Williams, an author with broadcasting experience, the 'recruitment officer'. Amongst his other duties Williams also began the investigation of press conditions in Germany, Austria and Czechoslovakia and held further responsibility for obtaining information from neutrals and refugees arriving in Britain.

Following Munich, plans for a propaganda department had been put on hold, but with the course of events a new urgency became apparent and Sir Campbell Stuart swiftly reactivated his 'Department of Propaganda in Enemy Countries'. This department was responsible to Lord McMillan, then Minister of Information. In order to build up the necessary stocks, for early use in any conflict, the Foreign Office had drafted the English text for some six different examples of leaflets, 'which were then translated into German by a mining engineer named Schmidt'. From these, the Permanent Under Secretary, Sir Alexander Cadogan, made a final selection and Her Majesty's Stationery Office duly prepared a print run of 10 million, at a cost of 6d per 100.

" One million one hundred and two—one million one hundred and three—one million . . . ."
Cartoon by Grimes. Reproduced by permission from " The Star."

Distributing aerial leaflets, a contemporary cartoon. (War Illustrated)

However, in Germany, despite the ruthless suppression of any opposition to the Nazi Party, home produced propaganda was already in evidence. An apparently innocent little publication entitled *First Aid in Accidents* was available in bookshops and contained an account of the Nazi persecution of the Church. *How to Play Bridge* might reveal a lecture on the means to pursue anti-Fascist work in Nazi organisations. Indeed, with the establishment of the German Freedom Party, open opposition to the Hitler regime had begun during April 1937, causing such aggravation to the Fuhrer that he was forced to declare it 'a foreign invention, born from a longing to see a split in our national unity'.

Frankreich und England
kämpfen
wie EIN Volk —
zu Lande,
zur See
und in der Luft!

„Die Stimme des deutschen Rundfunks, die England anklagte, den Krieg mit französischem Blut führen zu wollen, und so vergeblich einen Keil zwischen Frankreich und England zu treiben suchte, wurde übertönt von dem unaufhörlichen Dröhnen der englischen Truppen= und Artillerietransporte auf dem Wege nach unseren Grenzen."

Edouard Daladier 10. 10. 39.

„Es erfüllt uns mit Stolz, daß unsere Soldaten Seite an Seite mit den Soldaten Frankreichs stehen, deren Vaterlandsliebe, Entschlossenheit und Kampfgeist wir tief bewundern. Zwischen dem französischen und englischen Oberkommando herrscht absolute Einmütigkeit."

264
Neville Chamberlain 19. 10. 39.

'Frankreich und England'

Stocks of leaflets were produced for early use in the event of war. This example emphasises the unity between the French and English peoples. Trustees of the Imperial War Museum

Translation by Mrs R. Millington: France and England fight as ONE people – on land, at sea and in the air! "The voices which could be heard on German radio accusing England of fighting a war spilling French blood, and which vainly intended to drive a wedge between France and England, have been drowned out by the continuing roar of English troops and artillery supplies on their way to our borders." – Edouard Daladier 10 October 1939

"It fills us with pride, that our soldiers stand side to side with the soldiers of France, whose love of their country, whose decisiveness and fortitude of spirit we deeply admire. There is an absolute consensus between French and English high command." – Neville Chamberlain 19 October 1939

Electra House

As Chairman of Cable and Wireless, when Sir Campbell Stuart was appointed head of the Department of Propaganda in Enemy Countries, the organisation more usually took the name Department Electra House, Electra House being the headquarters of Cable and Wireless on the Victoria Embankment, London. The building had opened in 1933 as a new administrative headquarters for Imperial and International Communications, which then became Cable and Wireless in 1934. The previous headquarters, at Moorgate, remained as a centre of operations until bombed during the war, when activities were transferred to Electra House on Victoria Embankment. This building itself was damaged in 1944, when a flying bomb destroyed the Chairman's flat. (Cable & Wireless)

Below: Modern day premises in Blecthley. Cable & Wireless is now Vodaphone.

18

The Department of Propaganda in Enemy Countries was definitely a foreign invention, intent on the same aims. The headquarters was situated in Electra House, the headquarters of Cable and Wireless, on the Victoria Embankment, London. With Sir Campbell Stuart being the Chairman of Cable and Wireless, his propaganda department therefore acquired the more usual name of Department Electra House, more frequently abbreviated to 'Department E.H.'. In fact the Department occupied Room 207, complete with a Reuters tape machine and a wireless set. As a semi covert organisation, funding had been arranged from the Secret Vote by the Foreign Office but only on the express understanding that such activities were at all times conducted well away from Foreign Office premises!

Noel Coward had been secured for the Department's office in Paris and, in the event of war, close co-operation with the French would indeed be necessary. Thus Paris became the home of the 'Anglo French Propaganda Council'. After several visits, accompanied by both his private secretary, the French speaking Anthony Gishford and Lt. Col. Dallas Brooks, Campbell Stuart was hardly impressed with the liaison, and reported the attitude of his French colleagues as 'suspicious and superior'. In practical terms, he gained a far more useful assistance from his French Canadian relatives, not least his cousins the banking family of Beaulieu, from Montreal, who owned a banking house in Paris. Yet despite their respective attitudes, the joint Anglo/French arrangements for the printing of leaflets – to be carried by balloon – went ahead, albeit to criticisms by the French of the early British performance, complaining not only of grammatical errors but also of words wrongly employed as well. However, in a more positive direction, it was a French suggestion that initially recommended the investigation of bombs and shells as a means of leaflet delivery.

As the threat of war became inevitable, a relocation of the Department's headquarters from London to a safer refuge now assumed increasing priority. The Hon. Leo Russell, advertisement director of Illustrated Newspapers, a kinsman of the Duke of Bedford, suggested a move to Woburn Abbey. This was duly proposed, and the Duke, accompanied by Lt. Col. Dallas Brooks, by 'a gentleman's agreement', acquired the use of the Woburn Abbey Riding School for Department E.H., although after the Duke's death the organisation then swiftly took over the whole of the stately home. (Interestingly, despite his nationality Sir Campbell Stuart also had local connections with the immediate area, for his direct ancestor, eight generations removed, had been William Smith from Newport Pagnell, in Buckinghamshire).

David Bowes Lyon, brother in law of the King, was appointed as Sir Campbell Stuart's deputy at Woburn, and Department Electra House mobilised at 10a.m. on September 1st 1939. Staff were initially directed to the Sugar Loaf Hotel in Dunstable upon relocation. There they would ask for 'Mr. Gibbs Smith' (Michael Gibbs Smith, the Administration Officer). Nevertheless, for the meanwhile Sir Campbell Stuart, his personal staff, the chief printing officer and the military wing, under Lt. Col. Dallas Brooks, remained at Electra House whilst the Planning, Editorial and Intelligence sections settled into the Riding School.

Woburn Abbey

An aerial view that shows the Riding School, the long rectangular building. This became the early accommodation for Department Electra House but was demolished after the war. (Duke of Bedford)

Woburn Abbey, a present day aerial view (Mr. T. Trainor, Mr. P. Whitehead)

Vernon Bartlett became head of the Intelligence Department based on an early experience with the B.B.C. Talks Department, broadcasting in the 1930s from London and the European capitals,. However, he soon acquired a rather more immediate impression of Woburn when 'butted by a llama and bitten by a rhea', two of the rather frisky exhibits in the Duke of Bedford's somewhat exotic animal collection!

On September 3rd, the Intelligence Department of Electra House held its first meeting, and one significant result would be the regular issue of a 'News Digest', subsequently widely read in the Services Intelligence branches as a source of invaluable information. It was edited by Mr. Ireland, with a staff of 4. The 'Electra House News Digest' thus began publication on September 4th 1939 and eventually increased from a few foolscap sheets to a voluminous edition often exceeding 50 sheets.

On the day that the Germans invaded Poland, Sir Campbell Stuart was in Paris and, being of the opinion that his duties now lay with the Department in England, he hurriedly reserved places on the 4 o'clock train. He made swift arrangements to finalise his business in France at the Hotel Matignon, the Ministry H.Q., and consequently brought his French counterpart, Giraudoux, up to date on the propaganda activities. In a reciprocal measure, at the Hotel des Invalides, he in turn was then briefed on the latest French developments by Admiral Fernet. However, on returning to his own hotel, the Crillon, doubts now arose that the 4 o'clock train would actually run, and he urgently sent his staff on a desperate mission to secure the alternative of a car. Yet their efforts proved in vain, until the chance discovery of a black Hispano in the Place de la Concorde. A telephone call quickly confirmed that the Department had indeed transferred to the Woburn headquarters, (always referred to as C.H.Q., as the codename for Country Headquarters) and with necessary haste Sir Campbell Stuart and his entourage drove for the coast. At Boulogne the last sailing was scheduled for 7.30p.m. but, delayed by a puncture, the party missed their connection and instead headed down the coast to Dieppe, arriving with only minutes to spare. They eventually reached Woburn and discovered surroundings that were not entirely unfamiliar to Sir Campbell Stuart. As a small boy, in 1892 he had spent the summer with two great aunts in Aspley Guise, and on that occasion was taken as an especial treat through Woburn Park to see all the unusual animals. These were still a feature of the Park on his now more prolonged return.

Together with two or three close associates, as head of Department Electra House, he occupied quarters at Paris House, whilst other personnel lodged at 12 or so lesser dwellings in the village of Woburn, or in the immediate surroundings. The house in Aspley Guise, 'Woodlands', which after the war became Saint Vincent's school, was taken over by the Foreign Office to accommodate female typists employed at Woburn Abbey.

Visually stunning, as a late nineteenth century reproduction of a sixteenth century style, Paris House drew its name from having been directly transported from the Paris Exhibition of 1878, after there engaging the fancy of a contemporary Duchess of Bedford. Yet despite the architectural grandeur, as a place of residential accommodation Sir Campbell Stuart found the building 'inconvenient, dark, and depressing and in winter desperately cold'.

Place de la Concorde

On Departmental duties in Paris on the day that the Germans invaded Poland, Sir Campbell Stuart made swift arrangements for himself and his staff to return to England. With doubts as to whether the railway service would run, they commandeered a black Hispano car in the Place de la Concorde and made their escape. With the Fall of France, Nazi troops then became a familiar sight in the Place de la Concorde and even, on one occasion, a German aeroplane. (War Illustrated)

The Bedford Arms

Woburn, Bedfordshire—Bedford Arms
There are few places to stay at, and few who would wish to stay on Watling Street itself. But two miles off the trunk road adjoining the Duke of Bedford's estate, Woburn Park, is the Bedford Arms, a Trust House. Many times have I blessed Trust House organisation travelling between Northampton and London, for the location of the Bedford Arms. It is an oasis in a desert land. I know of nowhere else *en route.*

With many of the propaganda staff now settled in the Woburn area, the since renamed Bedford Arms became a favoured haunt for off duty relaxation. The extract is from 'Let's Halt Awhile', a 1943 guide, suggesting inns and hotels suitable for members of the Forces on leave. (J. Taylor Text: Let's Halt Awhile)

Most of the departmental work now took place at Woburn but with the military wing still retained in London, under Lt. Col. Dallas Brooks, Sir Campbell Stuart divided his time between the two centres. He would therefore travel for long weekends to Woburn, often in the company of influential visitors, arriving on Friday evening and returning on Sunday afternoon, accompanied in his Rolls Royce by three personal assistants and a filing cabinet! The problem of distance also tended to dilute the Departmental influence on the B.B.C., especially where this concerned the B.B.C. German Service, based in London. Matters, moreover, were hardly smoothed by the fact that the channel for conveying the Department's wishes and suggestions comprised two officers provided and paid for by the B.B.C.!

However, with Michael Gibbs Smith as the administration officer, Walter Adams as general secretary and Mr. Stewart Roberts (initially) responsible for finance, the 75 male and 43 female staff of Department Electra House duly settled into their new accommodation. This consisted of the stable wing of Woburn Abbey, and the Riding School and flats above the stable offices provided sleeping quarters. At the outbreak of war, 24 small cubicles were partitioned off along the 150 yards length of the Riding School and these all connected with a central corridor. Yet at least a measure of grandeur remained through the several works of art, stored for safekeeping in the building as an overflow picture gallery!

Paris House

Paris House became the residential accommodation for Sir Campbell Stuart, although he found it dark, depressing and cold! With the military wing of Department Electra House still located in London, he divided his time between the two centres, commuting in his Rolls Royce accompanied by three personal assistants and a filing cabinet! Later in the war, one of the most fascinating of the black propaganda radio stations would be that pretending to be run by an anti Hitler group of the Waffen S.S. Accommodated at Paris House, the speaker was indeed an actual officer of the unit who, having deserted, was smuggled to England by the Secret Service. (J. Taylor. Rolls Royce by courtesy of Mr. Needham)

23

The personnel now began their duties. They included many typists, recruited mainly from the Imperial Communications Advisory Board and Thomas Cook and Son, as well as 8 telephone operators, some from a previous employment at the Dorchester and Grosvenor Hotels. Catering was provided initially by J. Lyons and Co. and later by A.B.C. Nearly 10% of the salary bill regularly passed through the canteen till, perhaps hardly surprising since '5 sherries or a reasonable bottle of French claret' could be obtained for half a crown! Secrecy was paramount with no one allowed to give their address or talk about what they were doing and even letters had to be sent to London for posting. Constrained by such unorthodox conditions, perhaps for good reason at this time, the Abbey was said to have 'more than a touch of madness about it'. Yet measures for relaxing the tensions were being made, not least through the creation of a Recreation Committee in October 1939, which then dealt with such matters as finding a squash court and football field. They also arranged subscriptions to a local golf club, as well as seeking permission to ride hired horses through Woburn Park. The provision

Wolkiger Beobachter

As one of the early printed examples of propaganda, produced as a two page imitation Nazi newspaper, Wolkiger Beobachter was dropped over Hamburg, Bremen and Dusseldorf in November 1939. With the defection of Rudolf Hess, in May 1941, faked versions of the actual German newspaper, Voelkischer Beobachter, containing suitably altered pages, were planted for him to read, having been produced under conditions of tight security at the Luton News. Trustees of the Imperial War Museum. Translation (shown p. 26-7): (Mrs. R. Millington)

of a dance floor helped to further enhance the entertainments and in the Abbey, weekly cinema shows soon became a regular event. As a more work-oriented consideration, lessons in German were also arranged.

On the first night of the war, leaflets entitled 'A Warning to the German People' were dropped over Germany by British bombers. The leaflets bore a message from Chamberlain. This was repeated on the following night and that of September 6th/7th 1939, and again whenever weather conditions allowed. Of particular irritation to the enemy were the 'Truth Raids', flown by single high flying aircraft When the aircraft approached, the Germans were still obliged to deploy full A.R.P. precautions, lest the raiders were carrying bombs. Apart from aircraft, using a technique developed during World War One, balloons were also used to carry leaflets deep into enemy territory, and in the heart of the French countryside the first release was made on September 30th 1939.

Explaining his organisation as 'the fourth arm of offensive warfare', in November 1939, Sir Campbell Stuart arranged the formation of a Services Consultative Committee but, finding only a tepid reception, this ceased to meet in early 1940, although at a lower level contacts were still maintained with the armed forces. During this phase of the 'Phoney War' the main efforts of the Department were focused on the production of three or four varieties of leaflet, and on the night of November 6th/7th, 1939, the most prominent of these – a two-page imitation Nazi newspaper entitled 'Wolkiger Beobachter' (From the Clouds), a play on the name of the genuine German newspaper 'Voelkischer Beobachter' – was dropped over Hamburg, Bremen and Dusseldorf. On the night of January 13th/14th 1940, Prague and Vienna were then targeted for the first time.

For the manufacture of such productions, within the small hanger of the Woburn Abbey grounds, formerly used to accommodate the aeroplane of the 'Flying Duchess', in September 1939 two compositors from the University Press at Oxford had established a composing room. Here, set by hand in old fashioned German Fraktur type, they began to typeset the propaganda leaflets, and the early versions were then printed by rotary letterpress at H.M. Stationery Office, Harrow.

As for the effect of such productions, on one occasion a newly trodden path, leading into a forest, directed the German authorities to a tree, upon which had been pinned a leaflet! The German advance into Western Europe, plus the entry of Italy into the war, greatly increased the demands upon British propaganda, and accordingly the Woburn print unit relocated to Marylands, near Woburn village. Here, with Monotype equipment installed in an outdoor hut, the staff of the composing room was augmented to allow 24-hour working, and expert typographers and graphic artists greatly improved the quality of the work. Due to the volumes required, the actual printing now took place at the Luton based Home Counties Newspapers, as well as the Sun Engraving Co., Watford and Waterlows, Dunstable, who were specialists in photogravure. Employing colour, effective photographs could now be reproduced and this made for a far more sophisticated appearance. At the print works all the material was subject to a final

OBSERVER IN THE CLOUDS

About the first edition.

In Germany now, where everyone has a story to tell,
Where journals themselves only deceive,
Where everyone is forced into making confessions,
Where humiliation and shame grow hand-in-hand with lies,
Where many whisper who obeyed obediently, Where man and wife and children are left to plead,
Where wall and door are spying with their horrid ears,
Where people may lose courage,
Who would not be pleased in times like these – To see us bring the truth – and all that's new!

Between you and me.

To bring news of world affairs to the German people is an undertaking which does not in any way require an explanation or excuse. People abroad have for years been watching with heartfelt regret how such a great nation has become increasingly isolated under the Nazi terror rule.

The "Observer in the Clouds", however, believes nonetheless that our readers will appreciate a real newspaper, even if it is not delivered into your letter box, but dropped from the sky instead.

Goebbels and his boys.

The gunslinger journalist Goebbels and his green youths may have destroyed the proud profession of German journalism, but the very natural yearning for news of the thinking person cannot be quashed so easily.

A real newspaper.

So we are sending the number one edition of the "Observer in the Clouds", convinced that there are millions of upright German readers who will happily welcome a new newspaper, even if it's small; it will make a change to the usual stuff full of pathetic lies turned out by Jupp Goebbels and his ink splurging gang of weedy looking smart guys.

Our German readers want to know about the state of war – we will report on it. They want to know what the world says and thinks about Germany – the "Observer in the Clouds" will write about it.

From the Clouds.

Therefore, keep up your spirit, the "Observer in the Clouds" will continue to flutter down to you from high up in the sky.

Short News

Every week 2–4 German submarines are sunk! Finnland insists on keeping its neutrality intact.

Russia remains neutral.

During an air raid on an English convoy on 21 October, 7 out of 12 aeroplanes were shot down.

Winter Aid

In the main, Germany needs raw materials, such as fuel, manganese, wood, rubber, butter – and a new government and peace. As is reported by the Russian TASS-agency office stationed in the Reich's chancellery, the Bolsheviks promise that they will, in all probability, be able to supply fuel, manganese and wood.

All other goods will have to be procured in Germany itself and through the Germans' own efforts.

Lending Library (Illustration)

22nd September outside Warsaw

MAJOR GENERAL COUNT VON FRITSCH

Formerly Commander in Chief of the German Army
"killed" in action on the battlefield of honor .
Standing guard in sombre mood at the coffin of this great soldier
All soldiers of this World

SOLDIER'S HONOUR

Speech by a former English Guards Officer. Broadcast on English radio on 9th and 15th October 1939:

I speak as a soldier to soldiers. You Germans are a people of soldiers and I know that most of my listeners have either completed military service or are still under arms now. Professional soldiers are members of a big family, regardless of their nationality. Everywhere they are being trained equally hard and they all complain about their officer corps until they themselves become part of it. They always find something to criticise about the politicians they have to deal with.

The soldier must obey; he has to perform his duty. That goes for all soldiers and thus is only rarely that soldiers feel real hate towards one another. But even more important is the notion of chivalry, often described as the soldier's code of honour .

In the past I often had the opportunity to meet up will fellow soldiers belonging to the old German army. In the Friedrichstrasse barracks of the 2nd Guards Regiment I often dined with German military colleagues. Then in the autumn during a military exercise in Wurttemberg I shared my bottle of whisky with fellow German officers who were members of the Bavarian "Hunters".

What has always impressed me most about the German officer as such, has been his sense of fairness and chivalry.

During the World War I witnessed several incidents confirming this Impression, once a German officer firing a machine gun decided to stop shooting when he saw one of my comrades dragging a wounded soldier to safety behind the lines. On another occasion a German major refused to be taken back behind the lines until all his wounded men had been taken to safety.

Such memories make us ask what has become of the German soldier's honour when we hear how the brave General von Fritsch met his death. The rumour round here goes that he was murdered by Himrnler's Gestapo because he refused to introduce the National Socialist inspired contempt for God and corruption into the German army Whatever the truth, we cannot understand how your professional soldiers, how honorable former soldiers back from the front lines could tolerate the sombre farce of a state funeral for the best ever German general without putting up some resistance.

Because if Major General von Fritsch was not shot from behind by a murdering Gestapo sniper, then the jealousy and hatred of civilian non-soldiers sent him to his death.

I, for my part, have the duty to ask of the first captured German officer I encounter, what is meant by an "enforced reconnaissance backed by artillery". He should also tell me firstly how the Honorable commander of the 12th Artillery Regiment got into the most forward position on the battle line, and secondly how he could be killed like a common soldier during this peculiar military operation.

27

check and on one occasion, at the Sun Engraving works at Watford, a serious error was suddenly found regarding an important leaflet. The text mentioned a German rear admiral but the accompanying photograph featured another rear admiral of the same name! Millions of leaflets then had to be pulped and a new leaflet prepared.

For maximum impact it was imperative that the Department knew the enemy's state of mind, and towards this intention a large supply of German daily newspapers was organised through agents in the neutral countries. In fact by spring 1940, 90 German newspapers, trade and labour journals and periodicals, more than 100 allied and neutral newspapers from 16 different countries and a large number of the publications of refugee groups in Britain could all be referenced, having reached facilities in London soon after their publication. Employed by the relevant intelligence division, five linguists then studied the content, to decide which information might prove useful. From the European capitals the British missions telegraphed any news of importance and the B.B.C. monitored all significant broadcasts from enemy held territory, providing transcripts to Electra House. Many other sources also provided information but the availability of such intelligence disappeared abruptly with the speed of the German advance, in May 1940. Thereon, the British Legation in Stockholm received orders to buy every newspaper possible and have the R.A.F. fly them to Britain, once a week. Elsewhere, only German newspapers from Spain and Portugal could be obtained in a reasonable supply but often these would be out of date before they could be scrutinised.

Department Electra House also attempted to influence opinion in Germany via Germans resident in neutral countries, and, written by members of the staff, 'Deutscher' was consequently sent to the address of such individuals and business concerns. Department Electra House additionally had a few well placed agents in Switzerland and Belgium, and they would not only collect information but also infiltrate material into Germany.

As another form of propaganda, the Department had early realised the potential of rumour mongering to attack enemy morale, and perhaps the best known of the rumours was that suggested by Major White, at the time when a German invasion seemed imminent. This made it known that the British had a secret weapon which, over a vast area, could set the sea on fire and so destroy the invasion fleet. Somewhat more ridiculous was a suggestion that the British had imported 200 man eating sharks from Australia, to be released in the Channel! From the Air Ministry, an idea by Air Commodore Groves put out that German aviation spirit was of poor quality, and other ideas were also discussed, first mentioned in the records of the C.H.Q. at a meeting of the Undergound Propaganda Committee on 13th November 1940. Understandably, the Services wanted to know the effect of these rumours, and to accelerate their dissemination Mr. Cavendish Bentinck, 9th Duke of Portland, pointed out that the British Legations might be used. Also, by the suggestion of Valentine Williams, 'information' could be subverted into scientific and technical magazines.

As distinct from the approach employed during the First World War, apart from printed propaganda the potential of radio as an 'instantaneous' medium had become

Marylands

With the collapse of Europe, the need arose for increased volumes of printed propaganda. From accommodation in the former aeroplane hanger of the 'Flying Duchess', in Woburn Park, the Department's print unit then relocated to Marylands, once a cottage hospital, founded by the Duchess of Bedford. For the protection of the personnel an underground air raid shelter was built, which still exists - left. (Mr. B. Cairns, J. Taylor)

increasingly apparent. This was especially realised for 'black' wireless transmissions, as opposed to the 'white', truthful variety, by the B.B.C., and, subsequently dividing his loyalties between the two, as a senior figure at the B.B.C. Patrick Ryan thereby fulfilled the position of liaison officer between Department Electra House and the B.B.C. Indeed a Broadcasting Committee had been formed at Woburn on September 11th 1939, soon to be followed by a Joint Planning and Broadcasting Committee. Initially, this met daily, attended by representatives of the B.B.C. and the Political Intelligence Department.

Whaddon Hall

Under Colonel Richard Gambier Parry, Whaddon Hall became a headquarters for Secret Intelligence Service radio communications. In the early days of the war, propaganda broadcasts had been recorded in a makeshift studio in the gunroom and, as head of the technical operations from Whaddon Hall, Harold Robin began a consequent search for a suitable location in the district, where a radio transmitting station could be built. (J.Taylor, Vehicles by courtesy of Bletchley Park.)

Indeed, to assume eventual responsibility for the more covert transmissions, a former sales manager of the Philco Company, the 48 year old Colonel Richard Gambier Parry had been recruited, before the war, to improve the rather primitive state of the Secret Intelligence Service radio communications. The need was in fact well overdue, since most British Embassies had still relied on the diplomatic bag and postal and telegraph systems to maintain contact with London! At the end of 1939 Gambier Parry and Lisa Towse, his secretary and later his wife, accordingly moved into the designated headquarters at Whaddon Hall, a country mansion set upon an elevated situation. This had been requisitioned for the purpose by the War Office, and shortly to arrive was the Oundle educated Harold Robin who, throughout the war, then became responsible for all the technical aspects of the Secret Intelligence Service communications.

Robin began with the task of constructing a short wave broadcast transmitter convenient to Whaddon and, after surveying the immediate area, he selected a site in a large field near Gawcott, where two American 7.5KW transmitters were duly installed. Following on from a programme of previous recorded broadcasts, transmitted from elsewhere in the country, of a duration of approximately 20 minutes, the first propaganda broadcasts at Whaddon Hall were recorded onto 16 inch American glass based discs, in a makeshift studio in the gunroom. Played at 331/3r.p.m. these were then sent, via standard Post Office lines, for radio transmission from Gawcott. For the Germans, however, their recording technology was at this time rather more advanced, and for their own propaganda they had the significant advantage of early 'tape', or wire, recording, using the 'Tonschreiber', as a military version of the pre war 'Magnetofon'. This not only simplified editing but was also exempt from such giveaways of the recorded disc as needle jumping.

Gawcott Radio Station – A Wartime View

As the location to build a shortwave radio transmitting station, a suitable site was found in a large field near the village of Gawcott. From here the propaganda programmes, recorded onto discs, would then be broadcast. (Mrs. R. Mottram)

As the broadcast operations increased, so the need arose for more commodious premises, and Harold Robin and a colleague, Cecil Williamson, began a consequent search in the immediate area for a suitable centre. Literally by knocking on doors, they found an ideal location at Wavendon Towers, where the owner, Major Marler, was away in the army and, opting for a safer refuge, his dependents had prudently decamped to Scotland. Wavendon Towers had been built around the turn of the 19th century by the then Rector of Wavendon, the Rev. Henry Burney, as a wedding gift for his son, Colonel Henry Burney, who lived there until around 1915, and, following a succession of owners, Major and Mrs. Leslie Marler then bought the property in 1934.

Soon the secret broadcasters moved in and, codenamed 'Simpsons', from the proximity to a village of that name, under the charge of Ralph Murray four studios, including one in the billiards room, were soon organised. In due course Colonel Gambier Parry and later Harold Robin moved in and also accommodated were two recording technicians and three well-spoken young ladies, who supervised the arrival and departure of 'The Funnies', as the secret broadcasters were unofficially known.

From a short wave transmitter situated near to Woburn, on 26th May 1940, a day of National Prayer, the first programme in German was broadcast by Dr. Klaus Spiecker, an ardent opponent of the Nazis. A former civil servant under the Weimar Republic, he had fled to France before the war and duly established an anti Nazi radio station just outside Paris. On Sir Campbell Stuart's instructions, Terry Harman was then sent to investigate, and, aided by the French 2e Bureau, Harman met Spiecker and made arrangements for the Secret Service to smuggle him into Britain. However, as an effective offensive, propaganda broadcasts chiefly began after Department Electra House had been absorbed into the Special Operations Executive and the story is therefore continued in that chapter.

Wavendon Towers

With many new propaganda radio programmes either in operation or being planned, soon the need for a purpose equipped recording facility, as opposed to the makeshift measures in the Whaddon Hall gun room, became apparent. Wavendon Towers was chosen as the centre and here ultra modern equipment would be installed. As brother of the Queen, David Bowes Lyon, one of the members of the new organisation, arranged a Royal visit to the Woburn operations on November 19th, 1941. The visit was reported in the local press but not of course the nature of the activities. The King and Queen were shown around the various departments and listened to an especially made recording at the Wavendon Towers studio, where instead of using a visitor's book, guests made a recorded message of their arrival. (E.D.S. Ltd)

When Winston Churchill became Prime Minister, the position of Minister of Information was offered to Alfred Duff Cooper who, from the beginning of June 1940, then acquired control of Department Electra House. This thereby resolved Sir Campbell Stuart's uncertainty that 'since Electra House had had difficulty in getting the B.B.C. to do many things that they wanted, it should be determined who had the deciding voice in such matters'.

As the beginning of the end, 10 days after the Fall of France, ostensibly 'on business concerned with his duties as Chairman of the Imperial Communications Advisory Board', Sir Campbell Stuart, accompanied by Anthony Gishford and Captain Shaw, then embarked on a top secret mission to North America. Tasked to investigate the importance of British propaganda broadcasts from overseas, during his absence Valentine Williams now assumed control at Woburn and Lt. Col. Dallas Brooks held charge at Electra House. The mission not only secured for the B.B.C. the consent of the Canadian government to set up a shortwave radio station but plans were also proposed to broadcast direct from America to Germany, through either Newfoundland or Bermuda.

Yet despite these achievements, on his return Sir Campbell Stuart found little enthusiasm from the B.B.C., and, through being opposed by Lord Beaverbrook, Duff Cooper could wield little assistance. In fact the arrangements for propaganda would now dramatically change, for on July 16th 1940, Churchill invited Dr. Hugh Dalton, Minister of Economic Warfare, to take charge of a new organisation especially created for sabotage and subversion, the Special Operations Executive. The liaison officer between Department Electra House and Dr. Dalton's Ministry of Economic Warfare having been Leonard Ingrams, at a meeting of the War Cabinet on July 22nd 1940, Department Electra House then became absorbed into the new S.O.E. With Reginald Leeper in charge of the 'country operations' and David Bowes Lyon as his deputy, Sir Campbell Stuart now became surplus to requirements and had little option but to resign. Being Chairman of the Imperial Communications Advisory Committee, from August 17th 1940 he thereon devoted himself to this duty.

Sir Ralph Murray K.C.M.G., C.B.

Born in Partney, Lincolnshire, the son of an Anglican clergyman, Ralph Murray studied modern languages at Oxford before embarking on further language studies at various universities on the Continent. In 1934 he joined the B.B.C. and as European Correspondent covered the Nazi occupation of Czech Sudetenland and Austria. At the outbreak of the Second World War he then joined the planning service of Department Electra House and in due course became involved with SO1 and the subsequent Political Warfare Executive, helping to organise 'Black' and 'Grey' broadcasts to Germany, amongst other duties. He ended the war as Assistant Secretary, Press and Public Relations, for the Allied Commission for Austria. Soon after the war he was appointed as the first head of a Department set up to counter Soviet propaganda and in his continuing career held several diplomatic posts, including H.M. Ambassador, Athens, in 1962, the same year in which he was awarded the K.C.M.G. He retired from the Diplomatic Corps in 1967 and was appointed as a Governor of the B.B.C. From this position he retired in 1973 and eventually moved to Whaddon Hall, North Bucks, where he died in 1984.

(The Executors of Sir Ralph Murray)

CHAPTER THREE
THE SECRET BROADCAST RADIO TRANSMITTERS

In requisitioned accommodation around the district, each under the supervision of a British housemaster, teams of foreign exiles wrote and rehearsed their scripts for propaganda radio broadcasts. Accompanied by a censor, who usually lived with the team, they were then taken by car to a recording studio at Wavendon Towers, from where the resulting discs were transported by civilian drivers, in Secret Service cars, to the radio stations at Gawcott and Potsgrove for transmission.

GAWCOTT

As head of technical operations, then based at Whaddon Hall, in 1940 Harold Robin was asked to find in the near vicinity a suitable site for the construction of a short wave radio station. From here the propaganda programmes, recorded onto discs, could then be broadcast and, with his survey also encompassing the area around Buckingham, in a large field near the village of Gawcott he came upon the ideal site. Construction began and, approached by a gravel path, when complete the station was surrounded by a 4 foot high barbed wire fence, surmounted by an electrified wire.

Harold Robin

Born in 1911 in Streatham, South London, Harold Robin attended the technically oriented Oundle public school and, after studying at the City & Guilds Institute, joined the Standard Telephone Company, concentrating on adapting the design of American radios for British manufacture. He moved to the American firm of Philco in 1936 where the British sales manager, Richard Gambier Parry, would later recruit him for wartime duties with the Secret Intelligence Service. Initially his task was to locate sites suitable for shortwave transmitters in southern England to broadcast 'black' propaganda programmes and, moving to Whaddon Hall, he chose a site near Gawcott for another shortwave station. Throughout the war he remained in charge of the technical side of S.I.S. communications and became predominantly involved with the ultra powerful medium wave transmitter, 'Aspidistra', detailed in a separate chapter. (Mr. S. Halliday)

From pre-war employment in the Decca radio company, Thomas Pryke became the station commander, with Russell 'Rusty' Coleman as his deputy, and, for the various personnel, lodgings were found in the village. However, since some of the accommodation proved rather basic, many of the men preferred to shave at the station, which had the welcome provision of hot running water!

Gawcott Radio Station

Eventually to house two American R.C.A. transmitters, codenamed Geranium and Gardenia, built in 1940 the shortwave radio station at Gawcott would be used to broadcast 'black' propaganda programmes. Recorded on discs by teams of foreign nationals housed in the local area, in a highly secret operation the programmes were chiefly intended to give the impression of growing dissent within the occupied countries of Europe. (Mrs.R. Mottram)

Housed in a wooden building, there was at first just one transmitter - codenamed 'Geranium' – manufactured by the Radio Corporation of America, but, during December 1941 the Treasury sanctioned the purchase of an identical model. In consequence, pursuing the utmost urgency, as head of the Secret Intelligence Service communications Colonel Gambier Parry then sent off the necessary cable;

'A/C priority for the manufacture of a Model No. 4750, 7 1/2KW R. C. A. Transmitter'. This was for short wave operation in the 31, 41, and 49 metre bands and delivery was duly scheduled for April. Upon arrival 'Gardenia', as the codename, was then assembled in a brick building about 350 yards distant from 'Geranium'. Both were surrounded by brick blast walls and, in between, the incoming telephone lines for the site terminated in a smaller brick structure, which accommodated the office of Lieutenant Hal Fuller. Billeted in premises opposite the Lantern Café in Bletchley, he was also responsible for the station at Potsgrove and, whenever he was absent, Second Lieutenant Ainsley took command. Later they would both gain promotion, respectively to Captain and Lieutenant.

Personnel at the Gawcott Radio Station

The smaller, bespectacled figure is Thomas Pryke. Phil Luck, who replaced the engineer electrocuted at the station, stands on the right. (Mrs. R. Mottram)

Contained in separate brick buildings, two diesel engined generators could provide emergency power for each transmitter. Both engines were water-cooled, one being a Crossley and the other a Rushton with an eight-foot diameter flywheel. With a crowbar, this had to be set to a specified position before the engine could be started, using compressed air from a steel pressure vessel, kept supplied from a petrol powered compressor. Responsible for the maintenance of both engines was a three-man team headed by Bill Heatley, and they also maintained the two Rushton Hornsby models at Potsgrove. Working the same shifts as station personnel, men from the local Home Guard, including Jim Prickett, landlord of The New Inn, went about the various cleaning and maintenance duties.

For the actual transmissions from the station, the transmitter would be warmed up 10 minutes before a broadcast, with full power then applied two minutes before

Hillman Minx

The propaganda programmes were recorded onto discs at Wavendon Towers and the discs were then transported by civilian drivers, usually in black Hillman Minx cars of the Secret Service, to the radio station. The drivers were never allowed to enter or look into the actual transmitter room. Restored by Mr. G. Church, the Hillman Minx in the photograph represents an example that was used by wartime bomb disposal squads. The photograph was taken at the unveiling of the Milton Bryan studio commemorative plaque, on September 4th 2002. (J. Taylor)

the actual transmission. Protected in purpose made wooden boxes, the delivery of the propaganda broadcasts, recorded onto glass based discs at Wavendon Towers and later Milton Bryan, was the responsibility of drivers from a pool at 'Simpsons'. There, on December 12th 1941, Harold Robin reported that measures were being proposed to roof in the garage and include a chauffeur's room amongst the facilities. On Boxing Day Colonel Gambier Parry duly ordered a hut for the courtyard, but, for their canteen arrangements, in the early New Year came a recommendation that the drivers should eat at a local pub. However, the drivers – Weston, Vining and Newbury – favoured being paid an allowance to dine at home in the village and so, as a compromise, they gained an extra accommodation allowance of 5s a week, to pay for lunches out. From April 10th their pay was then increased to £4 5s.

When engaged on official duties, at this time it was also arranged with the Chief Constable of Bedfordshire, at Shire Hall, Bedford, that the drivers would be given priority if stopped. Their names and the vehicle registration numbers (two of these being CPW49 and FYP563) would be taken but the vehicles were not to be detained. Issued with passes to 'Simpsons' by P.I.D. (as the cover name for the P.W.E.) and to the transmitters by Colonel Gambier Parry, as at Potsgrove twice a day, in black Hillman Minx saloons, the drivers brought the propaganda discs to the radio station.

They had to arrive 30 minutes before the broadcast transmission and, even in the most atrocious of weather, never once did they fail, this despite during one period of adverse conditions an additional transmitter in the Cotswolds having to be used.

On arrival at the radio sites the drivers entered the transmitter building through a sliding door, which provided access to a cloakroom/locker room. This would be as far as they were permitted, for they were never allowed to enter, nor even look into, the transmitter accommodation. Each record was accompanied by a layout sheet which gave the programme number, transmission time or times, frequency and the number of the directional antenna array. An authorising signature also had to be present, without which no transmission could take place. Having repeated, in the relevant column, all the information on the card, confirmed by his signature, the engineer then handed over the discs from the previous delivery and waited for the driver to leave. Passing through another sliding door, providing access to the operations room here, facing the front panel of the transmitter at the operator's desk, he then sorted the discs into the order for transmission.

Adjoining the operator's room, a kitchen and toilets was situated on one side and on the other a workshop, complete with bench, hand tools and – in case of inclement weather or other emergencies – a bed, folding into the wall. In a final room was housed a large, oil cooled transformer where, by means of an autotransformer, the incoming supply of 220V was converted to 11OV, as required for American equipment.

Gawcott Radio Station

The operator's console, showing the radio equipment and turntable.   *(Mrs. R. Mottram)*

The aerials at Gawcott Radio Station

Diesel generators provided the station with an emergency source of electrical energy but in normal practice the transmitters drew power from the standard grid. During broadcasts, the output from the transmitters was fed via pole mounted feeder lines to the quarter wave dipole antennae array. A U.H.F. facility was also included, to allow emergency communication between the radio stations and headquarters. (Mrs. R. Mottram)

Leaving the daytime available for routine maintenance, due to the peculiarities of the atmospheric layers, transmissions were usually made during the evening or night. For these transmissions, via the relevant pair of knife switches, the output from the transmitter was channeled from the final stage of the equipment to pole mounted parallel feeder wires, which led across the field to the 1/4 wave dipole antennae array.

For 'Geranium', in contrast to the previous disc based activities, during 1943 the beginning of the renowned 'Soldatensender Calais' programme saw the live transmission of this broadcast direct from the studios at nearby Milton Bryan, linked to the Gawcott station by landline. On medium wave, Soldatensender would also be broadcast from the ultra powerful 'Aspidistra' transmitter, the site for which had been originally intended for Milton Bryan. However, primarily due to the concerns of the R.A.F., wary that the height of the masts would pose a hazard to aircraft flying from the local training airfields, a location was finalised instead on the South Downs. As for the smaller masts at Gawcott, similar concerns had been raised by the R.A.F. when a squadron of Mitchell light bombers began operating from nearby Finmere. Two officers were tasked to visit the Gawcott station but, in view of the prevailing security, they were not allowed anywhere near the buildings and had to conduct their enquiries from open ground, after which they were swiftly escorted back to the public road!

From late 1944, Gardenia was used to provide communications to S.H.A.E.F., employing Morse code on punch paper tape, delivered on rolls and fed at high speed through a 'Hellschreiber' machine. However, with the advent of new filters, connected to the incoming landlines, the coded information was then transmitted direct, eliminating the need for paper tape. After the war, Gawcott remained as a Government communications centre and only in recent years have the premises found a new employment, accommodating small business units.

POTSGROVE

Gawcott, the modern day appearance

Gawcott remained in use as a Government communications centre until recently. The premises now accommodate a number of small business concerns, but several of the original buildings still survive. (J. Taylor)

As with those at Gawcott, personnel for the Potsgrove station, situated a few miles from Woburn Abbey, consisted mainly of R.A.F. members on secondment, Special Communications staff and civilian G.P.O. employees. 24 hour working was maintained, with the shifts running 1700 to 2300, 2300 to 0800 and 0800 to 1700, two days leave being allowed every two weeks.

Assisted by Staff Sergeant Cox, the engineer in charge at Potsgrove was Norman Bowden and also included amongst the staff were Jack O'Connor, Jack Morton, Percy Jones and Bert Weatherhead. Percy and the two Jacks came from Special Communications Unit 1, whilst Bert had joined the R.A.F. and during peacetime owned a radio retail shop in Bletchley. However, early in the operation an unfortunate accident occurred at the station when an engineer named Locke, whose wife worked at the Wavendon Towers recording studio, was electrocuted. A safety feature on the equipment had failed to

41

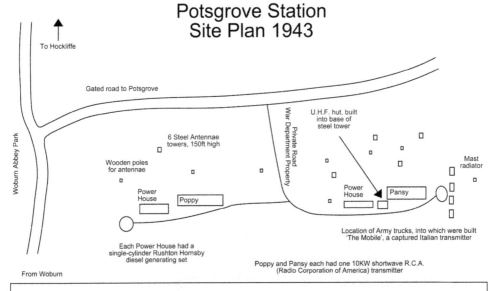

Potsgrove Station
Site Plan 1943

To Hockliffe

Gated road to Potsgrove

Woburn Abbey Park

War Department Property / Private Road

U.H.F. hut, built into base of steel tower

6 Steel Antennae towers, 150ft high

Wooden poles for antennae

Power House

Poppy

Power House

Pansy

Mast radiator

From Woburn

Each Power House had a single-cylinder Rushton Hornsby diesel generating set

Location of Army trucks, into which were built 'The Mobile', a captured Italian transmitter

Poppy and Pansy each had one 10KW shortwave R.C.A. (Radio Corporation of America) transmitter

---

Potsgrove radio station, a site plan, 1943

Prepared by Mr. Phillip Luck, one of the original station personnel, this plan details the layout of the Potsgrove radio station, as it would have appeared in 1943. Mr. P. Luck

Below: An extract from a secret log book, regarding a visit to the 'Pansy' radio transmitter at Potsgrove. (Mr. I. Murray)

7th November 1941

Mr. Halliday went to Simpsons to consult Mr. Robin regarding services available at Pansy (with a view to switching over the F l's as soon as possible) As Mr. Robin was not there Mr. Halliday let it be known that he was going to see Mr. Watton at the transmitter in the afternoon.

At 2.15 p.m. Colonel P. rang and requested Mr. Halliday not to visit the transmitter.

The reasons given:-

1. Mr. Murray had never done so.

2. He did not want his engineers concerned with the programme side, but solely with efficient transmissions. (Mr. Halliday explained that this was not a programme about which he wished to consult them.)

3. The whole question of policy was under review with Mr. Leeper at the moment, and until that was settled he did not want Mr. Halliday to visit the transmitters. Mr. Halliday told Colonel P. that if Mr. Robin had been there the questions could have been answered on the spot, but that as he wasn't then only did he wish to go to the transmitter. Colonel P. replied that Mr. Halliday should have telephoned him - the Colonel.

operate and, since the interlock on the transmitter's sliding access door was suspected as the cause, a manual earthing rod thereafter became a standard fitting, as a backup. Philip Luck was subsequently recruited as the personnel replacement.

For some of the staff urgently needed for their specialist skills, although they wore uniform they received no military training. Therefore, in the event of an incorrect salute, or other breach of military regulations, they had been issued with a Whitehall telephone number, a call to which would then have the matter quietly resolved!

A radio operator at the transmitter console

The propaganda programmes were recorded onto glass based discs and transported by car to the radio stations. There the technician placed them on a turntable ready for transmission. The discs were played at 33 1/3rd r.p.m., with the arm tracking from the centre to the outside edge. (Mrs. R. Mottram)

At the Potsgrove site two transmitters were installed, one known as 'Poppy' and the other as 'Pansy'. Initially 'Poppy' was equipped with only one turntable for playing the recorded broadcasts and, since none could be obtained locally, considerations to have one sent from the United States were made. However, to avoid this inevitable delay, Harold Robin instead arranged to have the turntable removed from the London Recording Unit, (probably located in Bush House). The standard for each transmitter was two turntables, allowing either for one broadcast to be made while another was being set up or to permit the extended length of a single broadcast. The records, the means of sound reproduction being made by variations of the groove width, were played at 33 1/3 r.p.m., with the stylus tracking from the centre to the circumference.

Before an actual transmission, the engineer would place a central mark on the record at a point on, or near, the beginning of the groove. The pick up arm would then be positioned on this mark and, with the operator listening through headphones, the turntable was set in motion. The operator then counted the number of revolutions

43

until speech began, and noted this number on the disc. By this procedure the operator could thereby bring the broadcast on air, without transmitting any 'hiss' from the stylus tracking in the groove during the few moments of preceding silence. The intention was to thereby convince the listening audience that the broadcast was live, but sometimes 'needle jumping' or 'ghosting', where speech from one track impinged on the next, could prove a problem, and transmissions were routinely monitored on the station's Hallicrafters communications receiver. The timing of transmissions was also crucial and an electric clock and a ship's chronometer ensured precision.

Wartime wireless equipment was necessarily large, using power-hungry valves. This example, only a few inches tall, is a modern battery- powered radio scanner utilising microchips and capable of receiving almost every frequency from 25MHZ to 1.3GHZ!

Especially regarding 'Aspidistra' – the ultra powerful radio transmitter purchased from America – anticipating the growth of future broadcast operations in December 1941, additional engineers, including Americans, came to Potsgrove to broaden their technical experience. However, in a quest for their local accommodation, Mrs. Stewart Roberts, of the administration department at Woburn, met quite a challenge!

In normal operation the radio station drew standard electrical power, but in case of disruptions to this supply, emergency generators, powered by a diesel engine, were installed. Yet even by early 1942 there was still no emergency diesel engine available for 'Pansy' and, to compound the situation, on March 5th the Potsgrove transmitter blew up, causing cancellations of the Fl programme. Urgent repairs were undertaken and, as an additional development in May, as a countermeasure to jamming, 'Poppy' was fitted with a multi-wave change facility, in fact a feature fitted to all four transmitters.

Around the local countryside, as evidenced by the mock battle staged at Woburn, in October 1941, the inevitable Army manouevres sometimes proved an unavoidable complication, as during March 1943 when, including a Czech unit, military personnel carried out an exercise in close proximity to the station. Transmissions then had to be held over, since the Army receivers would have been overwhelmed by the Potsgrove signal's output. In fact the station had an extensive array of aerials and on May 31st 1943, Harold Robin agreed for new 90 degree dipoles to be erected at Potsgrove, as required for 9 and 6 megahertz operation.

Despite the rural seclusion, the realities of war were brought home by the burial of a Flight Lieutenant at Potsgrove, killed on active service. Also on active service, Jack Turney, the rural postman for Potsgrove, was wounded in the 1943 North African campaign. In due course, helping in the preparations for D Day, the

'Soldatensender Calais' programme would be relayed from Potsgrove and in an additional measure, captured by the Eighth Army in North Africa, a mobile transmitter and audio station was prepared at Potsgrove for use by S.H.A.E.F., when the Second Front opened. The apparatus occupied four large British Army trucks, one each for the transmitter, audio studio, diesel generator and crew living quarters, but, although the equipment functioned well, new technological changes prevented the use for the intended purpose.

With the end of the war, the Potsgrove transmitters were put on a 'care and maintenance' basis and the personnel began to return to civilian life. Only four men now covered the three shifts and eventually just one sufficed, tending the premises by day and otherwise leaving the site locked and deserted. Open to the elements, the building that once housed 'Poppy' is now just a shell but little altered, that which accommodated 'Pansy' still remains, in company with the farmer's storage shed, which once saw use as the powerhouse all those years ago.

Potsgrove, the surviving buildings

Now derelict, several buildings still remain at the Potsgrove site. The long building accommodated the 'Pansy' transmitter, the shorter building housed the diesel generator and in between may be seen the U.H.F. hut. (J. Taylor)

TATTENHOE CAMP

For both the radio stations, billets in the near vicinity provided initial accommodation, but from mid 1944 staff were then centralised in a newly built camp at Tattenhoe, on the Bletchley to Buckingham road. Without regard to rank, meals were taken in a communal dining room, with the catering attended to by women of the A.T.S., supervised by Sergeant Steadman and Lance Corporal Lily Scott. Not only did they produce three wholesome meals a day but they also supplied haversack rations for those personnel working away on shifts.

At the camp, each hut had a central corridor with cubicles, some ten feet square, either side, furnished with a roughly made wooden wardrobe/cupboard and a single iron bedstead. Bedding – at least initially – consisted of a straw filled mattress, pillow and blankets. Electric tubular strips provided the heating, although this proved somewhat inadequate and a steam system was then installed instead, supplied from a large, solid

Tattenhoe Camp

Modern photograph of the location where, from previous individual billets, from mid 1944 personnel were centralised in a purpose built camp at Tattenhoe, on the Bletchley to Buckingham road. The on site entertainments of a bar and games room and the availabilty of three wholesome meals a day, prepared by women of the A.T.S., were a definite advantage. (J. Taylor)

fuelled boiler tended by 'Nobby'. He also fulfilled the role as barman and dispensed cigarettes and chocolate from the N.A.A.F.I. rations.

As a welcome contrast to the often lonely billets of the earlier years, on site entertainment included a bar, games room and reading room, with further amusements available further afield in the town of Bletchley. Transport to and from the various outstations was arranged by the Special Communications M.T. department at Little Horwood, and the comfort ranged from the relative luxury of Humber Super Snipe estates and Packards, to the wooden slatted seats of dark green Bedford buses and Austin 'Tilley' Utilities. Despite the incessant pace of 24 hour working, never once did the transport fail, nor the personnel be unavailable for their pick up.

After the war, with the camp demolished, the site became the location for a petrol station but today, as with much of the former countryside, newly built housing now overlies the area.

Austin 'Tilley'

Several types of vehicle were used to transport personnel about their daily duties, including the ubiquitous Austin Utility, or 'Tilley'. (Keith Coleman)

CHAPTER FOUR

SEFTON DELMER AND HIS IMPACT ON THE 'BLACK BROADCASTS'

Sefton Delmer, who was born and educated in Berlin, became the European correspondent of the Daily Express and thereby gained first hand experience of the Nazi rise to power. At the outbreak of World War Two, he fled to England and began working for British Intelligence by making secret broadcasts. His creation would be the first truly effective black propaganda station, 'Gustav Siegfried Eins', followed by programmes of equal success, specifically aimed at the German armed forces.

DENIS SEFTON DELMER

As the idea of Denis Sefton Delmer, during World War Two 'Gustav Siegfried Eins', abbreviated to 'GS1', became the first truly effective black broadcast radio station. Born to Australian parents in Berlin on May 24th 1904, Sefton Delmer, or 'Tom' to his friends, had been registered as a British citizen by the British Consul General. However, his father was interned at the outbreak of the First World War, although Sefton and his mother were allowed to remain at liberty. In May 1917, the whole family was then repatriated.

Sefton Delmer

Born in Berlin, as a Daily Express correspondent Sefton Delmer became well acquainted with the Nazis and their rise to power. Fleeing to England at the outbreak of war, after initial suspicions the Secret Intelligence Service offered him a role in the broadcasts of 'black' propaganda and several of the most successful programmes would then be his creation. Billeted in and around Aspley Guise, so many German P.O.W's and foreign nationals became involved in these activities that in just one week Mr. Tweedie, the dairyman of Aspley Hill, Woburn Sands, delivered over 400 pints of milk to the various premises!
(War Illustrated)

Delmer read modern history after winning a scholarship to Lincoln College, Oxford, and by reason of his father's publishing connections and through a chance meeting with Lord Beaverbrook, owner of the Daily Express, became that paper's Berlin correspondent in 1928. Bilingual in English and German, he was therefore ideally placed to witness and report upon the rise to power of Hitler and the Nazis. He was in Warsaw when the Germans invaded Poland, and had to flee the bombing of the city. At that time, aged 36, he sought a role with British Intelligence by reason of his experience and knowledge of contemporary conditions within Germany. Wary at first, the authorities declined his offer and in the meantime he continued his work at the Daily Express, also making occasional contributions to the B.B.C.'s German broadcasts. Indeed, his blunt and definitely unauthorised reply to Hitler's 'final peace appeal', flinging it back into the dictator's 'evil smelling teeth', caused quite a stir!

In September 1940, a friend with Intelligence Service connections then suggested that he should leave the Daily Express and begin work for secret broadcasting. This friend, of family associations with Barings, was Leonard St Clair Ingrams (nicknamed the 'Flying Banker', from his self piloted financial activities around Europe) and, with his suggestion receiving a favourable response, an interview with Valentine Williams, Reginald Leeper's deputy director for secret broadcasting at Woburn, then proved successful. However, it would not be until November 1940 that an oblique invitation arrived from the Intelligence Service offering Delmer, in the interim, an undercover role in Lisbon, using his Daily Express employment as a cover.

His task, in order to provide information on conditions within Germany, involved questioning those German Jews who were now leaving for America having bribed the Gestapo, but during these duties a telegram arrived from Ingrams. This requested that Delmer should resign from the Daily Express and return to England, where an important new job awaited him. Delmer duly returned in early 1941 and, although aware of his intended role in the Woburn operations, at first he had little to do except attend a few meetings and continue with his B.B.C. German talks. In March, however, he was given permission to establish a new right wing black broadcast station and his would be the vision that realised the advantage of talking to the mass of the German audience, not just a minority of ineffectual dissenters. His creation became 'GS1', signaller's German for Gustav Siegfried Eins.

GUSTAV SIEGFRIED EINS

With the outbreak of World War Two, in contrast to World War One there was no 'Liebknecht' in the Reichstag to express the opposition of the German masses, but dissent was nevertheless voiced by the broadcasts of the 'German Freedom Party', transmitting from a location, either within Germany or elsewhere, 'whose exact situation Herr Himmler would very much like to know'! The broadcasts began, 'Achtung! Achtung! Hier spricht der Deutsche Freiheitssender!' (Warning! Warning! The German Freedom Station calling!) and on October 15th 1939, the transmission was assumed to be coming from Cologne. Despite the uncertainty of the whereabouts, there were no doubts regarding the station's intent, as the following extract makes clear; 'In September Hitler told the German people there would never be another 1918. Yes, Adolf Hitler, there will never be another 1918. The work will be more thorough this time. German soldiers, make yourselves ready for the hour when you turn your guns round! Women of Germany, do your duty. German youth, become the flame of the revolution which is your honour and your destiny. Close your ranks for peace, freedom and bread.'

Yet with German military fortunes in the ascendant, it was realised by Sefton

Delmer that, however noble these sentiments, a more subtle and subversive approach was needed and for this he devised the 'black' propaganda radio station Gustav Siegfried Eins, signaller's German for George Sugar One. This revolved around 'Der Chef', (The Chief), a supposedly disaffected but otherwise loyal military figure and the part was to be played by a German born Pioneer Corps corporal, Peter Seckelmann. As the only member of the GS1 team to have arrived, in May 1941, he settled in at a secluded redbricked villa in Aspley Guise named Larchfield and here, as the top secret home of Delmer and his wife Isobel, began rehearsing the first of Delmer's GS1 scripts.

Larchfield, Aspley Guise

A secluded house in the village of Aspley Guise, for his wartime role initially Larchfield became the top secret home of Sefton Delmer and his wife, Isobel. In May, 1941, they were joined by Peter Seckelmann, who would play 'Der Chef' in Delmer's first black propaganda station, Gustav Siegfried Eins. (Mr. P. Thomas)

Always known at Aspley Guise as 'Paul Sanders', Seckelmann was born in Berlin in 1902 and became a city journalist. However, during Hitler's rise to power he grew so sickened by the increasing outrages against the Jewish population that he left for London in 1937 and started a small literary agency. In March 1940, he then joined the Auxiliary Military Pioneer Corps and eventually began training as a Special Operations Executive commando, thus coming to the attention of Leonard Ingrams. Delmer consequently became involved and, finding Seckelmann temporarily employed in a bomb disposal squad, made arrangements for his transfer to the secret broadcast operation, specifically as 'Der Chef' in the GS1 station.

Necessary to give a military authenticity by announcing 'Der Chef's' broadcasts, initially no 'adjutant' had been available for the programme, since the intended candidate,

Johannes Reinholz, who had fled from Germany with his wife, had yet to receive security clearance. However, with the sudden defection of Hitler's deputy, Rudolph Hess, rather than lose the opportunity to capitalise on this event, Delmer decided to go ahead anyway. Therefore on the afternoon of May 23rd 1941, he and 'Der Chef', Paul Sanders, in Pioneer Corps battle dress, were driven in a black limousine to the recording studio at Wavendon Towers, and that evening 'Der Chef' began his first broadcast.

Rudolf Hess

From the beginnings of the Nazi regime, Hitler and Hess became inseparable friends. As Hitler's deputy, when Hess flew to England on his mysterious mission, rather than lose the opportunity to capitalise upon this sensational event, despite there being as yet no 'adjutant' to announce 'Der Chef', Delmer went ahead anyway. This became the first broadcast of Gustav Siegfried Eins, in May 1941.

As an intriguing aside, eight days after the defection of Hess two German agents were parachuted into England near Luton Hoo. Found to be members of the S.S., they were interrogated and executed at the Tower of London, the nature of their mission having never been revealed. (War Illustrated)

Announcing the call sign, various messages in a low grade cypher then followed, in the certain knowledge they would soon be 'cracked' and send agents of the Gestapo pursuing all manner of futile 'leads'. After the initial announcements, 'Der Chef' then responded to 'questions', intending to create an impression that the station had been in operation for some time. Claiming a prior awareness of the Hess flight, he then gave a list of those arrested on suspicion, some of the names actually being correct. After the recording Jim Dougherty, one of the engineers, suggested that G3, as the code for the station, should have an identifying signature tune, and thereafter several bars from an 18th century folksong by Ludwig Holtz were employed.

Delmer's intention for the programme was quite clear; 'Our politics are a stunt. We pretend to have an active following to whom we send news and instructions. The purpose of this is to provide ourselves with a platform from which to put over our stuff'. Perhaps in view of his GS1 responsibility, a minute dated May 27th 1941 now decided that Delmer should assume joint control with Richard Crossman for the German department at Woburn, with Crossman having charge of the 'white' B.B.C. broadcasts, answerable to the Minister of Information. Yet in their respective approaches, Delmer and the Socialist Crossman differed completely. Crossman favoured addressing the mythical mass of 'good Germans' in an attempt to provoke a mass uprising, whilst Delmer, realising the folly of this, pursued his own unique line, via the format of GS1.

A UNIQUE OPPORTUNITY FOR BLETCHLEY
. . . PEOPLE . . .

MR. R. H. S. CROSSMAN, M.A.
Lecturing on . . .

"INSIDE GERMANY"

SENIOR SCHOOL HALL,
TUESDAY NEXT, JANUARY 16
at 8 p.m.

Chairman : Captain W. H. W. Ridley.

Preliminary Notice : Tuesday, January 30th :—
THE MASTER OF BALLIOL WILL LECTURE ON "WAR AIMS."

Later to become a famous post war Labour politician, Richard Crossman played an important role in the early propaganda activities. Advertised in a local newspaper, without revealing his actual duties he gave a local lecture on 'Inside Germany' at Bletchley in January 1940, at an event arranged by the Senior School headmaster, Mr. E.C. Cook, who had covert links with Bletchley Park. North Bucks Times

Stafford Cripps

In February, 1942, Sir Stafford Cripps, Lord Privy Seal and Leader of the House of Commons, was appointed to the War Cabinet. On methods of waging war he was not greatly impressed by the means employed by 'Gustav Siegfried Eins', describing Delmer's unit as 'that beastly pornographic organisation'! (War Illustrated)

During the early days of GS1, Seckelmann had not fully grasped the concept of the programme and, since this meant that Delmer had to rewrite much of the material, he was therefore especially relieved when the security checks on Johannes Reinholz were finally complete. Johannes and his wife then joined the GS1 team on June 5th 1941. The purpose of the GS1 station was to dishearten, demoralise and convince the German audience of a growing underground resentment deep within Germany, and upon this belief hinged the entire credibility of the operation. In the early days even pornography was employed and also language extremely offensive to the British, but, despite Stafford Cripp's disparaging dismissal of it as 'that beastly pornographic organisation', not surprisingly GS1 soon began to attract the interest of the intended audience!

For the content of the programme, valuable intelligence came from a radio operated teleprinter, left behind by a German journalist fleeing London at the outbreak of the war. This tapped the transmissions of the Berlin based D.N.B. (Deutsches Nachrichtenburo), the official German news agency, and thus press releases and Propaganda Ministry directives were often received and relayed by Aspley Guise before they even reached their official destination! For more personal details, these could be obtained from diaries taken from German casualties, and other sources included German newspapers and the interviews that Delmer had conducted in Lisbon.

On Radio Berlin, counter broadcasts against the British had been started by Hans Fritzsche, and Crossman asked Delmer to fashion suitable replies to the programme. On Thursday, June 6th 1941, Delmer was about to drive to London for this purpose,

Hellschreiber

Left behind by a German journalist, fleeing London at the outbreak of war, the Hellschreiber, a radio operated teleprinter, tapped the transmissions of the official German news agency and so provided invaluable information. (Mr. I. Murray)

when he received an urgent phone call from Leonard Ingrams, asking why he was not at Woburn Abbey. An important and highly secret conference had been convened but, not told of this, Delmer now drove hurriedly to the Abbey and in the ballroom found many important dignitaries, from military men to university dons, seated at long conference tables. Addressing the assembly, Reginald Leeper then announced that for several weeks Churchill and the Chiefs of Staff had known that around June 22nd Germany would begin an invasion of Russia, and the meeting had been arranged to decide how best to prepare the propaganda response. Taking his turn, Delmer confirmed that 'Der Chef' would be in full agreement and this was the direction that the programme would take!

As the GS1 broadcasts progressed, the team soon moved from 'Larchfield' to the more spacious 'The Rookery', which had been built in the 19th century on a plot of land opposite Manor Farm by the former Louisa d'Auvert, daughter of the Vicar of Haynes. For a while she had lived in one of the railway cottages owned by William Warr, a prominent farmer in the village, who in 1848 began to invest in property. When his elderly wife died in 1852 she then married him and, when William died, Louisa had 'The Rookery' built.

Here, whilst Mr. Maddy tended the gardens, his wife now acted as housekeeper, being taught French cuisine by Delmer's wife. As for more traditional fare, mushrooms could be gathered in plenty from the surrounding fields, free range chickens roamed the grounds and from the ducal estates even venison could be obtained. On a vast settee in the sitting room, Delmer often worked well into the night on his ideas and scripts and, perhaps for motivation, on display kept a shield inscribed with the words 'Hier sind Juden unerwünscht'. This trophy had supposedly been captured in Germany and then smuggled out in a sidecar!

In 1941 Ernst Adam joined GS1. Broadcasting from Paris, he had previous experience of working with a freedom station during the early months of the war and, having been on the Republican side in the Spanish Civil War, was also an experienced campaigner. However, his arrival at Aspley Guise had been somewhat delayed for, although the Special Operations Executive had smuggled him aboard a British cruiser, this was subsequently involved in the pursuit of the Bismarck! Alexander Maas was also brought in adventurous fashion to Aspley Guise by the Secret Service, and in fact he had been chief speaker and scriptwriter for the same Paris freedom station as Adam.

In August 1941 Max Braun then joined Delmer's team and he brought with him

Woburn Abbey, the ballroom

On Thursday, 6th June, Sefton Delmer was summoned to an urgent conference, convened in the ballroom of Woburn Abbey. Here it was announced that intelligence had been received regarding a German attack on Russia, planned for June 22nd, and the meeting had been arranged to decide the propaganda response. {Duke of Bedford)

The Rookery, Aspley Guise

With the expansion of the 'Gustav Siegfried Eins' programme, Sefton Delmer and his team moved from 'Larchfield' to the more spacious 'The Rookery'. In this aerial view the seclusion is apparent, slightly upper left from the church, in the top right hand corner. (Mr. T. Trainor, Mr. P. Whitehead)

much needed information regarding the current situation within Germany. A socialist leader who had led the anti Hitler front in the Saar, he escaped to France in 1933 and now at Aspley Guise, together with his brother Heinrich, a lawyer, he took charge of the intelligence department. Together they scoured obscure German newspapers for information and, assisted by contacts in Europe, began a card index on thousands of Germans. Other information came from intercepted mail, P.O.W. interrogations and possibly heavily disguised decodes from Bletchley Park. From November 1941, amongst the other GS1 personnel was 'Renee Halkett'. A thin, middle aged man, taken to wearing an eyeglass, his real name was von Fritsch, a cousin of the Commander in Chief of the German Army, but as an ardent anti Nazi he emigrated to England and then assumed the name of his Scottish grandmother.

By the end of 1941 the programme was enjoying increasing success until matters were jeopardised by one of the more notorious members of the operation, Freddy Voight. The son of a naturalised German father, he had been the Manchester Guardian's correspondent in Berlin and joined the British secret broadcasters at the suggestion of Sir Campbell Stuart. However, he deliberately leaked the truth about the GS1 station to the National Review and, when duly monitored by the Germans, they then ridiculed the programme in the weekly 'Das Reich'. Nevertheless, GS1 came back on the air after a few weeks and continued to make an impression on the German listeners. No action was brought against Voight and in later months he even wrote more articles that 'gave joy to Haw Haw'.

Early in 1942 Johannes Reinholz left GS1 and Frank Lynder then took over as the 'adjutant'. The son of a Bremen bookseller, his mother being Jewish he had fled from Germany in 1938 and in November 1941 Delmer interviewed him for the GS1 position. Accordingly, in January 1942, he travelled to Bletchley by train and, met at the station by Delmer, was taken by car to the Aspley Guise headquarters.

Until now, GS1 had been careful not to attack Hitler directly, an approach that could easily have been counter productive. However, in September 1942, when the moment was judged appropriate, 'Der Chef' began an oblique offensive, although maintaining Hitler to be a victim of corrupt, self seeking, party parasites, who swayed his decisions for their own objectives.

After only a few weeks, as the best service for

Alexander Maas

In 1941 Alexander Maas joined the Gustav Siegfried Eins team at Aspley Guise, having been intercepted abroad by the Secret Service.

(Mr. S. Halliday)

news and amusement, evidence became available that GS1 was being sought not only by U boat crews but also personnel in the highest of army circles. Indeed, according to an S.O.E. report from Sweden, GS1 attracted a larger audience than even the official German radio stations! As further emphasis, in December 1942, the interrogation of General Von Thoma then revealed that he believed the station to be in Germany, adding that the Gestapo had become so alarmed that individual reports were now being investigated.

Yet on occasion simple errors still threatened to reveal the true nature of the programme, as when another British station had been allowed to come on the air employing the same frequency. Nevertheless, even Goebbels was led to comment that 'Der Chef's' 'very close acquaintance with German conditions enabled him to invest his vulgar attacks with great verisimilitude'.

Eventually, with new British programmes planned or in operation, it was decided to fade out GS1 and in consequence, when 'caught' by the Gestapo, to the sounds of sub machine gun fire 'Der Chef' dramatically broke off in mid transmission during a broadcast in late October 1943. However, he actually died twice, since a non German speaking technician erroneously replayed the disc after the final episode!

'DEUTSCHER KURZWELLEN-SENDER ATLANTIK' (GERMAN SHORT-WAVE RADIO ATLANTIC) AND 'SOLDATENSENDER CALAIS' (SOLDIERS RADIO CALAIS)

The programmes of GS1 had been pre-recorded. Produced at the Wavendon Towers studio, the discs were then transported to the secret short wave radio stations at Gawcott and Potsgrove for transmission. However, as a progression from this, Delmer wanted to begin live broadcasts, which would convey current news in 'real time', embellished with popular music to attract the attention of listeners.

His embryo ideas now centred on two stations. One would be directed at the German army and the other primarily at U boat crews. Plans began to crystallise sometime before Christmas 1942, when, at his favourite London restaurant, Frascati's, he and those in authority conceived the idea of 'Soldatensender Calais', (Soldiers Radio Calais) and 'Deutscher Kurswellen-sender Atlantik', (German Shortwave Radio Atlantic). The need, especially for the latter, was now paramount, for by early 1942 shipping losses in the Atlantic were becoming catastrophic. Not least, the situation arose because of the Germans having introduced, from February 1st 1942, a separate key in their encipher machines for U boats. Whilst the so called 4 rotor Enigma – the naval M4 – did not actually have a fourth rotor due to the physical limitations of the case, the modifications produced the same effect, and Bletchley Park could no longer break the naval codes. Compounding the crisis, throughout 1942 the Germans had broken British Naval Cypher 3 and were now able to read the instructions sent to convoys.

The situation became so desperate that the Admiralty asked Delmer if there was anything that his organisation could do. 'Deutscher Kurzwellen-sender Atlantik'

U Boat

Captured U Boat personnel were employed on the 'Atlantiksender' programme, providing invaluable knowledge of the U Boat bases and methods of operation. Displayed at Bletchley Park, this mock up was recently used in a feature film. (J. Taylor)

therefore assumed initial priority, and perhaps it had been significant that naval personnel were present at the Frascatis meeting which conceived the intention. Lieutenant Commander Donald McLachlan, of Naval Intelligence, was authorised to offer the resources of the operational propaganda unit of the Admiralty, and variously during the war he would employ a local house, 'Woodcote', as his base. This had been sold to the Duchess of Bedford in 1903 for £4,000 and here she established her private physician, Dr. Glendining, who ran the Woburn Hospital.

When he unfortunately contracted T.B., with a supply of gas and water laid on she then had a wooden chalet built in the grounds overlooking the lawns, and here he spent his remaining days.

Another member of Naval Intelligence to become involved in the wartime secret activities, being a frequent visitor to Delmer's headquarters in Aspley Guise, was Ian Fleming, later of James Bond fame. In fact he early displayed a vivid imagination when he devised a daring plan to seize the German code books. He proposed infiltrating a captured German bomber into a returning flight and, within sight of the French coast, then simulating 'difficulties'. By suitable pyrotechnics attached to the structure, the appearance would thus be given that the aircraft was going down in flames and, when a German rescue launch arrived, commandos hidden in the fuselage would overpower the crew and seize the code books. The scheme was over-ridden!

For enhancing the authenticity of 'Atlantiksender', even broadcasting on occasion,

German refugees and P.O.W.s became intimately involved – although only after an intensive screening. Ten different announcers and six comperes, to introduce the music, would be employed, and the personnel also included at least ten petty officers of the U boat branch of the Kriegsmarine, who knew the latest U boat jargon and details of the U boat bases.

Involved with Naval Intelligence, Ian Fleming would often visit the secret broadcast headquarters at Aspley Guise, and no doubt gained valuable experience for his James Bond novels!

Initially the beginnings of the programme had been made with the assistance of the team from the 'The Rookery', Delmer's house in Aspley Guise, but soon extra houses in the village had to be requisitioned for the new staff arriving. In fact German nationals would come to occupy seven of the immediate premises. The new studio at Milton Bryan, (detailed in the relevant chapter), then became the centre of operations, and here one of the groups of German officers came under the charge of Captain Molly Fitzpatrick, an Irish woman.

After nearly a month of rehearsals and dry runs, on March 22nd 1943, introduced by a 'shrieking' pipe melody recorded on a Hammond organ by one of the more musical of the radio engineers, the station then broadcast its maiden programme. However, Delmer hoped to give the impression that the station had been operating for some time, thereby embarrassing the 'inattentive' German monitoring service, and indeed by the third transmission the enemy jammers were on. The programme enjoyed increasing success, as confirmed by the amount of 'Atlantiksender' material that found its way into the Swedish and Swiss press and thence to the newspapers of the free world. In fact, in the wake of the Dambusters raid, one fabricated story reported that farmers in the district of the Ruhr were illegally slaughtering their cattle for the black market, since the authorities could not distinguish between those that had drowned and those that had died from other causes.

Assisted on occasion by contributions from the American O.S.S., (equivalent to the British S.O.E.) attention could now be turned to 'Soldatensender Calais', which began broadcasts on October 24th 1943. Despite disagreements with the B.B.C., then using the transmitter to reinforce their European Service, Delmer gained permission to use 'Aspidistra', a powerful medium wave radio transmitter on the South Downs, for 'Soldatensender' from the night of November 14th 1943 between 8p.m.. and 11p.m., linked with short wave 'Atlantiksender' (G9). This he had first proposed on July 21st 1943 and, due to the ensuing success, the hours were then extended to midnight. At other times 'Atlantiksender' would go out locally on shortwave and, as proof of the effect, a passage from intercepted mail paid a welcome tribute; 'That thing is so cleverly done that friend and foe have just got to listen to it. It is as refreshing, commanding and appealing as anything I have listened to'.

The news was so accurate that the Gestapo began to investigate individual reports. Even Goebbels confided in his diary that 'In the evening the so called 'Soldatensender Calais', which evidently originates in England and uses the same wavelengths as Radio Deutschland – when the latter is out during their air raids – gave us something to worry about. The station does a very clever job of propaganda, and from what is put on the air one can gather that the English know exactly what they destroyed in Berlin and what they have not'.

Yet both stations were more 'grey' as opposed to 'black' and although not declared as British in origin, listeners may well have had their suspicions. Not that this mattered, for the accuracy of the news, with a slight distortion of disinformation, together with the captivating music (much of which – predominantly American jazz, with 'a German flavour' – was banned in Germany) continued to ensure a loyal popularity.

Milton Bryan

Linked to 'Aspidistra', a powerful medium wave radio transmitter on the South Downs, a purpose built broadcast studio centre was constructed at Milton Bryan during 1942. (J. Taylor)

Moleskin Fitz Patrick and her ricketty dog Spot.

Captain Molly Fitzpatrick

Involved in the Atlantiksender radio programme, one group of German officers came under the charge of Captain Molly Fitzpatrick. This caricature is by the architect of the Milton Bryan studios, Squadron Leader Halliday, who controlled the day to day running of the premises. (Mr. S. Halliday)

CHAPTER FIVE

THE SPECIAL OPERATIONS EXECUTIVE

After the Fall of France, by the merger of several covert organisations in July 1940, the Prime Minister, Winston Churchill, created the Special Operations Executive. Tasked to conduct sabotage and subversion in enemy territory and 'Set Europe ablaze', S.O.E. then took over secret activities that ranged from printed propaganda and radio broadcasts to the design and manufacture of sabotage devices and the training of special agents.

S.O.E. – THE BEGINNINGS

Following the annexation of Austria in 1938, several covert organisations distinct from the regular forces were hurriedly established for offensive operations. These included a section of the Intelligence Staff at the War Office known initially as GS (R) and then from around March 1939, as MI (R), Military Intelligence (Research), and under Colonel J. Holland this small department studied techniques of irregular warfare. Affiliated with an overseas base in the Middle East Command, known as G (R), the organisation positioned agents all over the world.

In addition to these measures, in March 1938 the head of the Secret Intelligence Service then appointed Major Laurence Grand, from the Royal Engineers, to create a new organisation, specifically to investigate 'non military' means of attack. These would include sabotage and 'black' propaganda, and the organisation went by the name of 'Section D', 'D' standing for destruction. However, for those not acquainted with the real purpose, they were led to believe it meant the Statistical Research Department of the War Office! Yet the secrecy was unknowingly compromised when Guy Burgess became the liaison officer between Section D and the propaganda department at the War Office! Nevertheless, from March 1939, authority was granted for Grand to send his agents into Central Europe and, by following the suggestion of Burgess, a few months later a specialised training school was set up to equip those operating under cover with the necessary skills.

By now Section D had a unit of seven persons involved in the preparation of black propaganda, producing printed material purporting to be of German or Austrian origin, some of which had even been infiltrated into Germany. In the winter of 1939 the headquarters of Section D then moved to 'shabby' rooms above St. Ermins hotel in London, but the propaganda team transferred to Woburn, theheadquarters of Department Electra House. However, they found no provision had been made to co-ordinate their work with the Department and, with Sir Campbell Stuart showing little interest in the 'black' side, they soon moved to a house in Hertingfordbury. There they remained for about a year, when a few transferred back to the 'white' section at Woburn.

As a result of the speed of the German advance, most of Section D's contacts in Europe were quickly overrun, and little could be done except leave dumps of sabotage stores which might eventually prove useful to an emerging Resistance. Indeed, in the face of impending invasion, Section D could now do little but organise 'left behind' parties across the British countryside which, from well concealed and supplied subterranean rooms, were intended to harass the enemy in hit and run tactics.

At this critical period Winston Churchill, recently appointed as Prime Minister, now urged the socialist Hugh Dalton to accept the new position of Minister of Economic Warfare for, as he poignantly observed, 'Time is pressing and it is a life and death struggle'. Indeed, with the German army poised across the Channel, the situation had completely changed and, on May 1st 1940, Dalton agreed to accept the appointment – actually a cover for the impending sabotage and subversion organisation. He accordingly asked Hugh Gaitskell, then in charge of Intelligence for Enemy Countries at the Ministry, to be his Principal Private Secretary.

At a meeting in the office of the Foreign Secretary on July 1st 1940, a decision was reached to form the new organisation for sabotage and subversion, which would replace the existing agencies and be headed by 'a controller armed with almost dictatorial powers'. On July 16th, Churchill sought Dalton for this appointment and at a War Cabinet meeting on July 22nd the new organisation came into being, to be known as the Special Operations Executive. This would then incorporate the former Section D, MIR and Department Electra House.

The public name for the organisation was 'The Inter Services Research Bureau', and for this new and additional role Dalton now acquired the secret title of Minister of Special Operations. He divided S.O.E. into three sections. SO1 acquired the propaganda role of the previous Electra House. SO2, as a combination of Section D and MI (R), dealt with sabotage, and, run by a Brigadier, SO3 attended to administration. However, after only a few months, this disappeared under the reams of paperwork and the staff were then found other jobs in Whitehall!

SO1 – THE POLITICS

At Churchill's suggestion, the Chief Diplomatic Adviser to the government, Vansittart, became Chief Adviser to the new special operations organisation and one of his first recommendations was to confirm Reginald Leeper, of the Political Intelligence Department, as the head of SO1, the propaganda arm. Despite being viewed by Dalton with some suspicion as to loyalty, Leeper consequently took charge of the 'country operations' of the former Department Electra House, with Valentine Williams as his deputy. However, Williams would leave in late July 1941 to represent activities at the S.O.E. office in New York, and from November 1941 his place was then taken by David Bowes-Lyon.

As the head of SO1, for his accommodation Leeper, accompanied by his wife and daughter, was given the Old Rectory at Woburn by Dalton, who had successfully blocked attempts to gain possession by the pacifist Duke of Bedford's equally pacifist housekeeper, Mrs. Samuel.

With the department nicknamed in Whitehall and Fleet Street as 'Leeper's Sleepers', the staff was soon increased to deal with the newly occupied countries in Europe. Accordingly, in August 1940, including the military section (under Lt. Col. Dallas Brooks) the London headquarters then transferred from Electra House, on the Victoria Embankment, to Lansdowne House, Berkeley Square, but Woburn, nevertheless, remained as the centre of operations. Here Leeper spent most of the week, usually hosting a 'tremendous house party' on Saturday nights at his home. After an excellent dinner, events were concluded with cigars and brandy, the assembled company being regaled with the views of Dalton or Dallas Brooks on the progress of the war. The following morning Dalton, 'a great booming bully', would then delight in taking, or perhaps coercing, 'volunteers' from his immediate entourage on a long country walk, often breaking into a jog, although 'Some responded better than others to this form of recreation'! Yet despite often being cast as a bully given to shouting aggressively at subordinates, it was said that if he was being genuinely unreasonable and the minion shouted back, then Dalton would usually back down with good humour.

In the new organisation, finding no appointment offered to him, Guy Burgess went back to the B.B.C. and became a producer in the Talks Department. However, by this position he retained links with the propagandists at Woburn and perhaps not surprisingly, tried to influence their views into the pro Soviet cause! As for Kim Philby, he was assigned to the teaching staff of the S.O.E. sabotage school at Beaulieu, in Hampshire, and, tasked with the propaganda aspects of the curriculum, he also had links with the Woburn propagandists, often visiting the Abbey. As for the Department's staff at Woburn, Dalton initially had the majority returned to Lansdowne House, in London, near his own ministry in Berkeley Square, but the onset of German bombing

6 Leighton Street, Woburn

As Principal Private Secretary to Hugh Dalton, whenever the Minister was absent from Woburn Hugh Gaitskell exercised supervision. After his London quarters were bombed out, Gaitskell then acquired the tenancy of 6, Leighton Street, Woburn, for the purpose. After the war, Gaitskell pursued a political career and became Leader of the Labour party. (J. Taylor)

soon caused a speedy retreat to Woburn within a month, excepting the small military wing headed by Dallas Brooks. Whenever absent from Woburn, Dalton exercised supervision through his capable secretary Hugh Gaitskell, who had first come to his attention as a young socialist at Oxford. After his London quarters were bombed out, for local convenience Gaitskell then acquired the tenancy of 6, Leighton Street, in Woburn.

Thus now back at Woburn Abbey, the propaganda section (SO1) continued to deal with subjects such as policy guides for the European Service of the B.B.C. and leaflets dropped by the R.A.F. In fact an early question of principle had concerned airborne leaflets – were they overt or covert? Ruled to be covert, they thereby became the responsibility of Dalton, which caused friction with Alfred Duff Cooper, the Minister of Information who, having charge of overt propaganda, considered that Dalton encouraged a left wing bias in the C.H.Q. (Woburn) productions. Attempting to resolve such tensions, on May 16th 1941, Anthony Eden, the Foreign Secretary, called a meeting with the Lord President, Sir John Anderson, to seek his arbitration, and perhaps the impartiality of Anderson is best gauged through his comments on the question of conscientious objectors, stating that 'No person should be penalised for the mere holding of an opinion, however unpopular that opinion might be to the majority.' The 'Anderson Award' consequently devolved responsibility for secret propaganda to Dalton and overt to Duff Cooper. As the respective heads of the Ministries of Economic Warfare and Information, for joint control of the co-ordination they would then consult with Eden, as the Foreign Secretary. For practical management each party would appoint an official to co-operate at the working level, and on June 16th Eden appointed Robert Bruce Lockhart of the Political Intelligence Department, although

Anthony Eden & Sir John Anderson

Tensions between the Ministers in charge of propaganda, regarding their areas of respective responsibility, led to arbitration being sought by the Foreign Secretary, Anthony Eden, from the Lord President, Sir John Anderson. The resulting 'Anderson Award' produced a compromise solution but not until the later formation of the Political Warfare Executive did matters become fully resolved. (War Illustrated)

he only agreed on the understanding he would be made a Deputy Under Secretary. Reginald Leeper represented the Minister of Information and Dallas Brooks, as a key figure in SO1, the Minister of Economic Warfare. In all matters Eden had the final word. During the same month, Dalton and Leeper invited Leeper's deputy at Woburn, Valentine Williams, to represent SO1 in America, and at a salary of £3000 pa. for an appointment for six months he duly arrived in New York on July 28th 1941.

Despite the new agreement Duff Cooper, encouraged by elements of his staff, continued to press for a full control of propaganda and to this effect had even written to Churchill. He put his case to the Cabinet on June 24th, when his arguments proved not only in vain but also saw him shunted off the scene altogether, as the following month Churchill proposed him for 'an important mission' in the Far East. Brendan Bracken then became his replacement. Yet unrest still continued and, after much discussion in the Cabinet, Churchill initialled a new Charter for propaganda warfare in August 1941. As a Standing Ministerial Committee, this now provided for regular meetings between Eden, Dalton and Brendan Bracken, and an operational committee was set up under the chairmanship of Robert Bruce Lockhart, as the Foreign Office representative. At the end of August the ministers agreed to so act as a trinity and duly established an Executive Committee of three officials who, in addition to Lockhart, were to be Reginald Leeper and, as Lockhart's deputy, Brigadier Dallas Brooks. On September 10th 1941, incorporating the former role of SO1, the control of the new organisation was finally approved. It would be known as the Political Warfare Executive, and the following day the formation was publicly announced in a ministerial answer to a parliamentary question put by Commander King-Hall, M.P.

Brendan Bracken

The 'Anderson Award' had devolved responsibility for secret propaganda to the Minister of Economic Warfare, Hugh Dalton, and overt propaganda to the Minister of Information, Alfred Duff Cooper. Yet the latter still tried to press for full control and was shunted off to a Far Eastern appointment by Churchill for his troubles. Formerly the Prime Minister's Private Parliamentary Secretary, Brendan Bracken then became the new Minister of Information in July 1941. (War Illustrated)

SO1 – THE PROPAGANDA

In order to broadcast a shortwave 'black' radio programme to Germany, from May 1940 Department Electra House had established an early, if primitive, propaganda recording studio in the gunroom at Whaddon Hall, the walls being crudely draped with soundproof material. However, when SO1 took over, following the Fall of France, the need then soon arose for more sophisticated facilities, and Harold Robin, head of the technical side of the secret communications, together with a colleague, Cecil Williamson, eventually chose Wavendon Towers as the new centre, near to Woburn. Here several studios were set up and shuttered and curtained; one would be in the billiards room

Dawn Edge, Aspley Guise

Various houses of the district were requisitioned as accommodation for the 'Research Units', groups of foreign nationals engaged in secret propaganda broadcasts. Dawn Edge housed the G2 team, of the 'European Revolution Station', with the socialist politician Richard Crossman as their housemaster. Other houses included The Heath, Broomdown, Netherfield House and Woodlands. (J. Taylor, by courtesy of the owner)

where, beneath the novel introduction of fluorescent lights, three chrome plated R.C.A. microphones awaited use, one suspended from the ceiling, one on a stand and the other mounted on a desk. Later the billiard room would find use as a waiting room for those broadcasters waiting to speak, but, compromising the secrecy, the walls were not soundproofed. Occasionally this then led to rather unfortunate incidents when one team, representing a particular political position, could hear the broadcasts of another, representing a different political view!

With the duties of Department Electra House now absorbed into the SO1 branch of the Special Operations Executive, it would be under this consequent control that the broadcasts became an effective operation, recorded onto 16 inch American glass based discs and played at 33 1/3r.p.m. German, Italian and French teams were now lodged within separate houses of the immediate region, and, in the following weeks, unsuccessful offers were also made to Mr. Darsie Gillie, head of the B.B.C. French Service, to take charge of a French 'Freedom Station'.

With Reginald Leeper presiding, on August 31st 1940, at the first meeting following the formation of SO1, plans were discussed for an 'International Communist Station' which, as a Marxist station, broadcasting on 31.3 metres, would urge the German workers to abandon Fascism and encourage European goodwill. The Communist theme was however abandoned and the programme began from October 7th as the 'European Revolution Station', G2, (Sender der Europaischen Revolution), written by a team called the 'Neubeginn'. From internment camps on the Isle of Man, several speakers had been 'recruited' and, run by a group of German socialists, the station would transmit a total of 582 programmes. Yet feedback from German prisoners of war proved the programme had little effect, and many Germans remained unaware of the station. Settled at 'Dawn Edge', Aspley Guise, the members of the team came under the charge of the later politically famed Richard Crossman as housemaster, although he caused constant problems for the security officer by always referring to 'Simpsons' as Wavendon Towers! Well favoured by Dalton, although not greatly accepted by Leeper, Crossman became head of the German department at Woburn in August 1940 and there he stayed until May 1943, when assigned for duties in Algiers at the headquarters of General Eisenhower.

By this time a Romanian and an Italian R.U. had also been started and, during the course of the war, at one time or another some 60 stations were in operation. During late November 1940, the French 'black' station Radio Travail duly began, in company with Radio Inconnue, and eventually Travail would broadcast 551 programmes and Inconnue 1145. With Mr. Kingsbury as housemaster, The Old Rectory (now demolished) at Toddington provided accommodation for the script writers and broadcasters, and, similarly requisitioned in the local area, the pattern became for other teams to also live in a suitably sized house, under the charge of a British housemaster. He would supervise their work and daily life, whilst his wife normally attended the domestic duties. The teams were never allowed to divulge their work, or use the telephone or telegrams without permission. They were also forbidden to visit the local pubs, although on more than one occasion the landlady of The Anchor, in Aspley Guise, had cause to verbally restrain certain amongst her customers from lapsing into their native tongue!

The Anchor, Aspley Guise

Many teams of foreign nationals, engaged in the various 'black' propaganda radio programmes, were accommodated in houses of the local district. They were expressly forbidden to visit the local pubs but nevertheless, on more than one occasion the landlady of The Anchor had to ask that certain of her customers stop lapsing into their native tongue! In more serious incidents, a pass to the recording studio at Wavendon Towers was found in a local pub and also a pass to the radio transmitter stations. (J. Taylor)

Functioning independently of each other, the 'freedom stations' were given the general cover name of 'Research Units', since unwelcome visitors calling at the house were invariably told that the new arrivals were engaged on secret research work. Even tradesmen engaged on the routine maintenance were always kept under escort.

Accompanied to the recording studios by a censor, who usually lived with the team, he would vet the scripts and, by means of a cut off switch linked to the microphone, ensure that only the authorised versions were broadcast. Staff of the different R.U.s (supposedly!) never met and, driven to the recording studio by civilian chauffeurs, the cars, usually a black Hillman Minx, made use of a complicated series of shuttles to ensure that each journey was made in isolation. Yet, despite these precautions, the system had failings and, as previously mentioned, on one occasion broadcasters of a certain nationality overheard the broadcast of a separate team in adjoining studios. As another annoyance, despite a strict no smoking rule, one R.U. became notorious for leaving their cigarette ends in a smoke filled studio. Due to the lessened thickness of the peripheral material, each team was asked to limit their recordings to 12 minutes on disc. However, they very often exceeded this allocation and, because of the resulting poor technical quality, the overrun could not be transmitted.

A letter of the alphabet identified the target country for a broadcast team. Thus F stood for France, Y Yugoslavia, B Belgium and X Bulgaria, although as a politically incorrect exception Italy was designated W, for Wop! (Perhaps some antipathy was understandable, since an Italian P.O.W. engaged on local agricultural work had nearly decapitated a member of the escorting Home Guard with a scythe. After a prolonged chase, the prisoner was shot dead.) Only under emergency conditions were the R.U.s permitted to broadcast live, and in normal operation discs recorded at Wavendon Towers would be taken, by car, to the radio transmitting stations at Gawcott and Potsgrove. Here, obtaining a sufficient number of wooden poles for the wireless aerials had initially posed a problem, since the right to fell any fir trees on the estate had been refused by the somewhat pacifist Duke of Bedford. Indeed, of his views regarding Hitler, the Duke had said "I see him as an 'untested' man of mixed attributes, whom it is neither necessary, sensible, or right to quarrel with until he has been tested by the one test which to me is worth anything – that of wise, practical, genuine friendliness." However, the day after the Duke's death, in August 1940, Gambier Parry then sent workers out at first light to cut down as many trees as they needed!

Apart from the covert broadcast operations, on March 12th 1941 there appeared in London the first issue of 'Die Zeitung', the only free and independent German newspaper in Europe. The editors were the anti-Nazi journalists Dr. Lothar and Dr. Haffner, the latter having been the author of the two books, 'Offensive against Germany', and 'Germany – Jekyll and Hyde'. The leading article of the newspaper explained the aim as being to assist 'in rallying all the resources, physical and moral, of the Free Germans on behalf of Britain', calling on them to join with all the Czechs, Poles, Dutch, Belgians, French and Norwegians fighting for their liberation, for 'the British Isles have become the bastion not only of the Free British Commonwealth, but of European freedom'.

As for the secret propaganda radio stations, the most effective would be 'Gustav Seigfried Eins', the creation of Sefton Delmer, as revealed in a separate chapter. The role of SO1 was absorbed in August 1941 into the Political Warfare Executive, and soon afterwards a new purpose built and ultra modern broadcast studio was constructed at the village of Milton Bryan, a few miles from Woburn. As the man in charge, largely from his experience with GS1 during the SO1 period, from here Sefton Delmer would direct the 'black broadcast' operations to even greater effect.

SO2 (ACTIVE OPERATIONS)

A t the creation of the Special Operations Executive the responsibilities of Section D were now shared. The 57 year old Frank Nelson, educated at Bedford Grammar school, who had worked for the Foreign Office in Switzerland until the Fall of France, gained joint responsibility with Laurence Grand.

Grand was now asked by Dalton to arrange a special mission to France to rescue a fellow socialist politician, Leon Blum, but Grand replied that he would have to seek approval from the War Cabinet, before risking lives on such a non priority assignment. When Dalton refused, in the ensuing standoff Grand was sacked, being 'damned glad to return to ordinary soldiering'. His removal now allowed Nelson to carry out a purge of the former Section D, and as head of SO2 Operations and Training he chose Colonel Colin Gubbins for the appointment, from the previous MI

Major General Colin Gubbins

Colonel Colin Gubbins was appointed head of SO2, the active operations side of S.O.E. In 1943 he then took charge of the organisation.

Tempsford Airfield

In this barn, which still survives, secret agents were issued with equipment for their clandestine missions. The stone ledges on which the equipment was stored may still be seen. On certain nights, it is said, the engines of the waiting Halifax aircraft may still be heard. (J. Taylor)

(R). In fact Gubbins would eventually be appointed head of S.O.E. in 1943.

For active operations, late in 1941 No. 138 Squadron, R.A.F., was formed at Tempsford in Bedfordshire, and from here agents would be flown out on secret missions, these duties being also shared by No. 161 Squadron. As for one of the pilots, he acquired a locally inspired nickname by crashlanding his Westland Lysander in Whipsnade Zoo, being thereafter universally known as 'Whippy'!

For communication with their agents overseas, S.O.E. initially had to rely on the radio network of the Secret Intelligence Service, but from mid June 1942, linked to S.O.E. headquarters a separate wireless organisation then began, maintained by four home based S.O.E. signal stations. Two were locally situated at Grendon Underwood and Poundon, respectively codenamed 53A and 53B. Grendon Underwood already had experience of enemy activity when, reported by the police and a local farmer, at 3am on the night of June 26th 1940, two high explosive bombs had been dropped near the village, killing two cows. For the S.O.E. operations, the large house at Grendon (now used as an open prison) came under the command of Major Phillips and employed personnel on a range of duties from cipher clerks to radio operators. Poundon House came under the command of Major Adams and additionally communicated with an S.O.E. training school based in Canada – S.T.S. 103 – instructing American agents. A station at Bicester, 53C, also operated from April until November 1944, whilst, at Thame Park, the S.O.E. radio school taught operators to transmit Morse code at 25 words per minute. In conjunction with P.W.E., S.O.E. was also involved in a black broadcast radio station, 'Radio Patrie', which first transmitted on October 8th 1942. This provided a direct link with organised French Resistance and on May 9th 1943 was

Poundon House

A wartime signal station, codenamed 53B, for the Special Operations Executive. (J. Taylor)

Chicheley Hall

As Special Training School No. 46, at Chicheley Hall, Czech and Polish agents underwent sabotage training. (Chicheley Hall Conference Centre)

replaced by a new station, 'Honneur et Patrie', which relayed all the orders and directives of the Conseil de Resistance, based in London.

Another means of attacking enemy morale employed the use of 'sibs', or rumours, and, nominated to join the Joint Intelligence Committee as head of the SO2 representatives, Captain Sheridan then attended the weekly meetings of the Undergound Propaganda Committee at Woburn. 'Sibs' were also forwarded to the Committee by SO1, Ralph Murray being included amongst the members. By the suggestion of Mr. Barry, of C.H.Q. planners, sibs were also linked to the R.U.s, and eventually Radio Inconnue, addressing mainly the 'petit bourgeois class', became the most effective.

Conceived at 'The Firs', a large mansion situated at Whitchurch, various sabotage devices also played a major role in harassing the enemy including a small, easily concealed incendiary package known as a 'Braddock'. Initially the idea had been that of Winston Churchill, inspired by a John Steinbeck novel, and with instructions for use, they were to be dropped by air for the benefit of the Resistance and foreign workers. However, the R.A.F. refused to carry them and instead they were supplied to Delmer, on the understanding they might, by now, be 'stale'. Indeed they were, as Delmer discovered when testing an example on the lawn at 'The Rookery', Aspley Guise. Even when he put the device on the fire it didn't burn! Yet nevertheless, those planted by agents achieved their objective, helping literally to fuel suspicion amongst the foreign workers. In a further measure, urging travellers to tear out suspect fittings in case they hid such devices, S.O.E. agents on board German passenger trains also disseminated fake notices. In fact fake documents, of exceptional quality, had become a speciality of Delmer's 'black' printing unit, set up by an expert typographer, Ellic Howe. Many such productions were thereon supplied to S.O.E. agents and were also included in arms drops for agents deployed in the field, and of local note, it would be revealed after the war that Mrs. C. Maude, of Chestnut Farm, Drayton Parslow, had been one of those trained to be a resistance leader, although perhaps not at Chicheley Hall.

For the training of S.O.E. agents, by June 1941 Special Training School No. 46 had been established at Chicheley Hall, near Newport Pagnell, where, by May of the following year, Czech agents were undergoing instruction. In July 1942, it came under Czech authority, with Polish agents included for sabotage training by March 1944. From April 1944, the Hall then became used as a wireless telegraphy training school for F.A.N.Y.

CHAPTER SIX

THE POLITICAL WARFARE EXECUTIVE

Disagreements and disaffection, between the various ministers and their staffs vying for the control of propaganda, caused not only problems of morale but also of effect, and in 1941 the Prime Minister, Winston Churchill, initialled the charter for a new organisation. This would be called the Political Warfare Executive and from thereon British propaganda would achieve spectacular – if covert – success, in operations that ranged from counterfeit documents of exceptional quality to hoax radio broadcasts for deceiving the German population.

THE BEGINNINGS OF P.W.E.

After much discussion in the Cabinet and often bitter argument in the Commons, the Prime Minister, Winston Churchill, had initialled a new agreement for the regulation of propaganda warfare in August 1941. This provided for regular meetings between Anthony Eden, the Foreign Secretary, Hugh Dalton, the Minister of Economic Warfare, and Brendan Bracken, the Minister of Information. It also set up, under the chairmanship of Robert Bruce Lockhart, (a Foreign Office appointment), an Executive Committee. The three Ministers duly agreed to work as a trinity and, at the end of August 1941, the proposed Executive Committee of three officials was then established. In addition to Lockhart, also included were Reginald Leeper and as Lockhart's deputy, Lt. Col. Reginald Dallas Brooks, confirmed as head of the military wing.

On September 10th 1941, the day that the structure of the new organisation was formally approved, Robert E. Sherwood, a playwright and personal acquaintance of the U.S. President, Roosevelt, paid a timely visit to Woburn as head of an equivalent body, the American Foreign Information Service. The visit had been arranged by his friend, Lockhart, and during the tour he was informed not only about P.W.E. but also received copies of recent leaflets and details concerning many of the current 'R.U.s', the secret broadcast stations.

With due deference to secrecy, on September 11th, the day after approval, the formation of the organisation was then announced to the Commons, David Stephens being appointed as the organisation's Secretary. The name, the Political Warfare Executive, had been the idea of one of the members, David Bowes Lyon, who had suggested the title in preference to the previously offered Political Warfare Organisation. However, very soon the department became unofficially known as 'Pee Wee' and the officials as 'Pewits'!

By the very nature of the work little could be made generally known about the department, and from the autumn of 1941, P.W.E. assumed the cover of P.I.D., employing Political Intelligence Department notepaper and advising the address as 'P.I.D. of the Foreign Office, 2 Fitzmaurice Place, W1'. As Chairman, Robert Bruce Lockhart now assumed responsibility for the entire organisation and in particular for maintaining contacts with the Foreign Office, who had the final say on all aspects concerning foreign policy. In this new appointment he therefore established himself in the Locarno Room of the Foreign Office and began gathering his new organisation about him in London, although the 'black' activities remained at Woburn, being deemed too secret and sensitive to move.

On September 17th 1941, the first meeting of the three Ministers and the three officials of the Executive Committee took place at the Foreign Office, the idea being that at these meetings the Executive Committee would receive guidance and approval from the Ministerial Committee. The new arrangements did much to calm the propaganda scene but tensions still remained. Bracken tried to establish both a geographical and ministerial control whilst the Woburn organisation, led by Dalton, nurtured a reluctance to relocate. Indeed, on his first visit to Woburn as Chairman of the Executive Committee, Lockhart met with immediate threats of revolt and resignation and not surprisingly came to regard himself as little more than a link between the Ministers and the 'lieutenants'.

Notwithstanding his many other pressing concerns, the Prime Minister now had little option but to again give the matter his consideration, and in consequence a further agreement for managing P.W.E. was proposed, reducing the number of Ministers from three to two. In February 1942, this was achieved by a neat solution, whereby the Prime Minister appointed Dalton as President of the Board of Trade, so extracting him from the realms of propaganda and subversion altogether. He became aware of the news during a visit to his constituency, attending a Warship Week engagement at Shildon, and, speaking directly to Churchill from the confines of an air raid shelter, upon confirming the Prime Minister's confidence in his ability for the job, duly accepted the position.

The Locarno Room

As Chairman of the newly created Political Warfare Executive, Robert Bruce Lockhart initially administered the organisation from the grandeur of the Locarno Room at the Foreign Office. The Locarno Pact had been signed in the room on December 1st 1925, hence the name.
(The Wonderful Story of London)

Under this new arrangement with only two ministers, Eden became responsible for policy and Bracken for administration. As for Lockhart, answering to his patron, the Foreign Secretary, on matters of foreign policy and to the Minister of Information on operational concerns, although now elevated to the position of Director General he hardly enthused about his impending role; 'So now I am sole boss of the whole show; I feel no exhilaration'.

The previous fortnightly meetings of the two committees of ministers and officials were now abolished and, at the end of February 1942, Lockhart and Dallas Brooks moved their respective sections from the Foreign Office and Fitzmaurice Place to accommodation directly above the B.B.C. European Service in Bush House. Here, for the first fortnight, the staff then mainly survived on a menu of 'coffee and kippers'! P.W.E. could now win a better control over policy and broadcasting output, as agreed by the B.B.C. Governors and, strengthening this liaison, Lockhart appointed Ivone Kirkpatrick, Foreign Advisor to the B.B.C., as a member of the P.W.E. Executive Committee.

The complete story of P.W.E. lies beyond the realms of a local book, but nevertheless many P.W.E. activities were carried out from the immediate area and their tale is told in the following pages.

Bush House

Home of the Overseas Service of the B.B.C. in 1942, those elements of P.W.E. not involved in the secret broadcasts or the typeset and design of 'white' leaflets were transferred to Bush House, in London. The diminished threat of enemy bombing had been partly the reason but with the onset of the German V weapons campaign, in 1944, a near miss caused damage and casualties, when a V1 flying bomb exploded in the Aldwych. Plans were then made to relocate the organisation back to Woburn Abbey, if necessary. (The Wonderful Story of London)

THE MOVE TO LONDON

With the diminished threat of bombing, as early as November 1941, a recommendation had been made that staff involved in policy making and with the B.B.C. 'white' broadcasts would move to London, whilst those engaged in secret broadcasting and the production of white leaflets, typesetting and design, should remain at Woburn. Indeed, the Woburn section might be said to have received Royal 'approval', for, through the influence of David Bowes Lyon, an official visit to the

Woburn organisation by the King and Queen was arranged on November 19th 1941. They were then shown around the various premises and informed about the nature of the activities.

THE KING AND QUEEN.

——o——

VISIT TO WOBURN ABBEY.

The King and Queen paid a private visit to Woburn Abbey on Wednesday. Travelling by road, they entered the park by the London entrance. Mrs. Bowes-Lyon accompanied them. Capt. Bowes-Lyon, the Queen's brother, was also present. They lunched at the Paris House, and were shown over the Abbey.

The visit by the King and Queen was reported in the local press, although without revealing the propaganda activities!
(North Bucks Times)

As for his assessment of certain members of the Woburn staff, Lockhart's opinion of Reginald Leeper, his former Foreign Office boss at P.I.D. and now the head at C.H.Q. (Woburn), was somewhat unflattering. Thinking him 'already overpaid, though I would be prepared to pay him more as a pension', even in October 1941 Leeper still enjoyed a free house, car, petrol, entertainment allowance and £3750 per annum. Lockhart, meanwhile, had to find his own rent, was allowed no car or entertainment allowance and earned a salary of only £2000 per annum. The fact that Leeper sent his Rolls Royce four miles every day to fetch milk from a local farm, may also have compounded the bias! It therefore seems ironic that one of Leeper's first activities at Woburn was to set up a P.W.E. committee for agricultural propaganda!

Soon after settling in at the London headquarters in Bush House, accompanied by Lockhart, on Tuesday, March 31st 1942, Brendan Bracken, Ronald Tree of the Ministry of Information and Lord Birkenhead travelled in Bracken's Bentley to Woburn, in accordance with Bracken's desire to visit the establishment. Being a wet and miserable morning, their inspection began at the Abbey where, with Leeper acting as guide, they viewed the large rooms and picture galleries that now accommodated the main offices of the 'country section'. Bracken, however, showed more interest in the art treasures than the occupants, although he became more enthusiastic at Marylands (which housed the Production Unit) and also the black broadcasting activities at Wavendon Towers. The party then adjourned for dinner at the Old Rectory.

Having concerns about the distance from London and the consequent high consumption of petrol, on the way back in the car Bracken spoke to Lockhart about returning more of the staff of the 'country establishment' (Woburn) to London, except for those engaged in the really secret activities. Tasked with an immediate

With the role of Department Electra House absorbed into the Special Operations Executive, David Bowes Lyon became deputy of the Woburn propaganda operations. As the brother of the Queen, he invited their Majesties to tour the local facilities, and for their benefit a broadcast recording was especially made at Wavendon Towers. Indeed, the Queen and her brother had connections with the local area since their mother, Lady Strathmore, was the daughter of the Rev. Charles Cavendish Bentinck, who had been vicar of the parishes of neighbouring Husborne Crawley and Ridgmont (church shown above). In the year of her marriage, Elizabeth was inadvertently reacquainted with the area when, travelling with the Duke of York – her future husband – on their way from London to attend the Pytchley Hunt, their car broke down at Battlesden, on the road between Hockliffe and Little Brickhill. An A.A. Scout telephoned a local garage and they then continued their journey in another vehicle. (J. Taylor)

enquiry, in fact Lockhart had already been engaged in similar discussions regarding the re-organisation of P.W.E. intelligence. Most intelligence material, under the existing arrangement, was initially routed through Woburn, where that for the exclusive use of the R.U.s would be retained and the remainder then sent on to London via six telephone lines and a teleprinter service. This meant, however, that P.W.E. often lacked the complete intelligence necessary for their plans, and in consequence, at the Saturday morning meetings at Woburn, matters were often independently dealt with that should also have been the province of meetings at Bush House.

In view of this, an argument for a move could be made, not least to allow access to the vast amounts of intelligence that had been gathered in the press cutting and filing library at Woburn. This information would then prove useful to the B.B.C., who had their separate News Information Bureau in Bush House. Nevertheless, for the meanwhile the Woburn organisation continued their duties, and on August 17th 1942, Ritchie Calder, assisted by Lord Birkenhead, was appointed the Director of Plans and

Campaigns for P.W.E., operating from 'the ducal china closet' in Woburn Abbey. A bed-sit in the village provided his off duty accommodation.

With Lt. Col. Metherell as his assistant, Mr. Meikle then became Chief Administration Officer of the department, and his responsibilities would assume an added urgency from November 7th 1942, when Bracken reaffirmed his views regarding the organisation's high petrol consumption. Accordingly, on December 24th 1942, Meikle recommended that Lockhart should accept a P.W.E. report on the subject of a move, prepared by Brigadier Eric Sachs, and, as Director General, Lockhart duly spent a long day at the office with his administration officer, going over the details.

As a result, by the end of the year most of the non essential staff had been transferred from Woburn to Bush House, but, as Director of P.W.E. 'Country', Leeper bitterly opposed the move. Regarding 'the country' as more conducive to thinking and planning, he had nevertheless anticipated the outcome and sent a private letter to Lockhart, stating that he now wished to return to the Foreign Office. Lockhart discussed the matter with Eden, and on January 7th 1943, Leeper resigned, accepting a new appointment as Ambassador to the Greek Government in exile. From January 11th 1943 Tom Barman deputised.

THE WOBURN ACTIVITIES: PRINTED PROPAGANDA

By the move to London, P.W.E. relinquished Woburn Abbey and in the local area now retained only the Riding School, Marylands, Milton Bryan and the R.U. and administration houses. The Woburn activities were therefore reduced to 'black' and 'grey' broadcasting and the layout and setting up of 'white' and to a much lesser extent black printed propaganda at Marylands. Here, with the art department, writers and typists accommodated in the dining room, the staff, including some five art directors, (two of whom were American), worked under the direction of Harold Keeble, Head of the P.W.E. Production Unit. Before the war he had been the art director of Beaverbrook Newspapers. Yet at least in the upheaval the facilities hadn't suffered. In well equipped print shops at Marylands, favouring the more expensive rotagravure method, (as being more professional for photographic reproductions) the work of the unit was received from the writers and translators at Woburn Abbey. This was then laid out, set up and proof-read by language experts, being then delivered to outside contractors for volume production.

Responsibility for the staff, the preparation of menus and similar matters fell to Mrs. Todd-Thornton, whilst the efficient running of the typographical machinery became the responsibility of Tim Tyler. A marvellous camaraderie existed amongst the staff that included several Americans, sent to learn from the British expertise after America's entry into the war. Prior to Pearl Harbour, in the form of the Co-ordinator of Information Department the United States had anticipated the possible need for such activities. However, when this became a reality, such was the desperation to learn from the British experience that one of the Americans destined for Marylands had actually been 'swopped' for a destroyer! Primarily the American interest was in the production of airborne leaflets, and to convince the U.S. Air Force of this importance a 'beautifully made' brochure entitled 'Paper Bullets' was produced in London, with Harold Keeble much involved in the project.

As for 'black' printed propaganda, since the specialised equipment only existed in London, this became the centre for such operations, carried out under the direction of Ellic Howe. Assisting his efforts an expert forger was especially released from jail, since he could reproduce a perfect signature of Adolf Hitler!

In the days of Department Electra House and S.O.1, the early examples of 'black' had been of insufficient quality to pass a close examination, and it was indeed fortunate that Ellic Howe had arrived at the opportune moment. A professional typographical expert, whilst serving as a sergeant at the H.Q. of Anti Aircraft Command he had written a paper on the subject but, with this being turned down, a year later he then resubmitted his views. His report quickly attracted the attention of P.W.E. and, invited to join the organisation, working initially under Leonard Ingrams from November 1941 he then became involved in a small postal unit, producing forged stamps and associated items. He also attended the weekly meetings at C.H.Q., Woburn, but was dismayed to find that no systematic plans were in place. He thereon built up his own independent outfit, investigating the London print trade for the necessary firms and equipment suitable for the work. Sefton Delmer became so impressed by the quality of the productions that he began providing the unit with an increasing number of projects, arguably amongst the most effective being that of a 'malingerer's handbook'. This showed, by graphic illustration, how workers and military personnel could feign illness and thereby be 'legitimately' relieved of their duties!

Aircrew & leaflet drops

Early leaflet drops had not been a great success, aircrew having to leave their station and hand feed the leaflet bundles through the aircraft's flare chute. Not only were the results often inaccurate but in hostile skies it was also highly dangerous, especially if the rear gunner was tasked to leave his turret. (Britain's Wonderful Air Force)

Leaflet drops sometimes caused almost as much physical as psychological damage, a bundle on one occasion smashing a hole through the roof of Notre Dame Cathedral!

'Le Courrier De L'air' (Trustees of the Imperial War Museum)

By contrast, separate from those printed productions intended for the enemy, the 'News Digest', originated by Department Electra House, had now acquired an avid readership amongst the Intelligence departments of the Services. Reflecting this popularity, the first printed edition, as opposed to the previous 'Roneoed' copies, appeared on November 28th 1942.

By now the amounts of printed propaganda produced by P.W.E. were substantial and, to actually deliver these increasing amounts over enemy territory, reliable means and mechanisms became essential. Bundles thrown out by aircrew on leaflet missions had not achieved unqualified success, for one package managed to crash through the roof of Notre Dame cathedral whilst another holed a German barge, sinking the vessel! Few aircraft could be spared in the early years of the war for dedicated leaflet drops, and such missions were therefore mainly confined to Operational Training Units of the R.A.F. The specialised S.O.E. squadrons sometimes offered assistance but, even so, during the early months of 1942 the average air release of material, mainly 'Le Courier de L'Air', was under 400,000. This compared with the 2 million desired by P.W.E. However, sympathetic to the P.W.E. ideals, the Americans often provided aircraft for the purpose and were also instrumental in the development of a specialised leaflet bomb.

By 1943, with Harold Keeble, from the Daily Express, as the kingpin of the P.W.E. print operations, some 50 versions of leaflets a month were being produced in 10 languages, at a cost of £9,000,000. Suitable leaflets advertised the 'black' broadcast stations, whilst fake issues of the German army news- sheet, Skorpion West, were also made. The forgeries even included ration cards. Dropped by aircraft on bombing missions, the radar blinding 'window' also played a part, the aluminium strips printed to appear as propaganda leaflets and so divert attention away from the intended purpose.

Detailed in a separate chapter, especially for the Invasion one of the most important of the P.W.E. propaganda productions was a newspaper intended for the German troops, 'Nachrichten für die Truppe'. As Sefton Delmer's idea, this brought up to the minute news of events, otherwise denied or heavily censored by the German authorities, and by the combined efforts of an extensive staff, working from hurriedly erected pre-fabricated accommodation, the contents were written at Milton Bryan.

PROPAGANDA RADIO BROADCASTS

Apart from the printed word, in the form of radio broadcasts the spoken word was also an integral part of P.W.E.'s local activities. Indeed, before long the output of the various R.U.s became so prolific that, weighing nearly two tons, some 3000 records had been produced, with those records now redundant routinely transferred, in boxes, to the pigeon loft at Woburn Abbey!

Many new stations were now in operation or being planned including, from November 21st 1941, that for G5, following discussions at Delmer's home, 'The Rookery', in Aspley Guise. However, the following day it had been decided to cancel Libya as the proposed target in favour of the Eastern Front, but even by the end of the year the station had not begun operations, since one of the team members was awaiting transport, by bomber, from America.

Two Belgian stations operated in close co-operation with the Belgian Surete and, with the co-operation of General Sikorski, another R.U. transmitted news intended for Polish agents in Poland and Germany. This would then feed the pseudo German clandestine newspapers. As for the actual effect of the R.U.s, when four of the names that appeared in a 'gallery of traitors' were broadcast by a Bulgarian station, within a year all had been eliminated.

The Mount

The house was demolished in 1964 and new housing now overlies the site. In 1942 the premises accommodated members of French broadcast teams but in 1944 was the scene of an unhappy tragedy. A maidservant became pregnant by a Police War Reservist and, while the balance of her mind was disturbed, she strangled her male child and hid the body in a suitcase. The father of the child refused her any help and, when the crime came to light, the maidservant was bound over for two years and ordered to enter a religious community home, under the care of the welfare authorities. (J. Taylor)

On January 24th 1942, the French teams for F1 and F2 were moved to 'The Mount', Aspley Heath, and it was intentional policy that the broadcast teams were always kept separate, in terms of accommodation and recording. By this means unintentional copying of ideas and techniques could be avoided, although exceptions did occur. On one occasion, just as the F2 team was leaving 'Simpsons', they were hurriedly recalled when some important news broke. Their return happened to coincide with the arrival of another team proclaiming their de Gaullist cause and, although the studios were supposed to be soundproof, through the thin back wall of an open fireplace the French Socialists heard the opposition in full flow. At once they all resigned!

Also in operation, another French station, F3, 'La France Catholique', had begun on July 1st 1941 with Capitaine Lagrave as the speaker. He felt, however, that he should be more involved in active operations and the station subsequently closed on May 14th 1942, when he left to train as a pilot in the Free French Air Force. Nevertheless, a few months later the Air Ministry agreed that he could work for P.W.E. two or three days a week and the station thus reopened on June 3rd 1943 with a Breton priest, Capitaine 'Perfi' Florent, as his assistant. He would also broadcast during his absence. Later Lagrave fell ill and, being declared unfit for flying duties, then returned to a full time occupation with P.W.E. As already mentioned, most of the teams of writers and speakers for the R.U.s were housed separately but, again concerning the French, one exception was that of the young Gaullist soldiers of the French station, F4, and the French priest who ran F5. He lived in the same house and was thus able to attend to their spiritual needs from a 'chapel' set up in a bedroom!

For use in the R.U. operation, Sefton Delmer explored every manner of weird and wonderful theme including, on March 9th 1942, an Occult Station (G6), with Harold Robin asked to allocate a frequency and arrange a recording session! On air from September 15th 1942, one R.U. then purported to be in Germany, run by Father Andreas, a bearded refugee German Catholic priest, and his theme emphasised the impossibility of serving both Christ and Hitler. Amongst the other unusual stations, from early 1943 the Wehrmachtsender R.U. picked up German D.N.B. broadcasts on the wallmounted Hellschreiber in the teleprinter room at Milton Bryan, and so transmitted current news before this even appeared in the general press. In fact most of the items were true – with a few false trails thrown in!

Pere Florent

Capitaine 'Perfi' Florent, a Breton priest, became the assistant to Capitaine Lagrave, the speaker on one of the French propaganda radio stations. Lagrave left to train as a pilot in the Free French Air Force but, falling ill, then resumed his broadcast duties. (Mrs I. Murray)

Father Andreas

A refugee German Catholic priest, he ran a radio station, purporting to be in Germany, that emphasised the impossibility of serving both Christ and Hitler. (Mr. S. Halliday)

For a first hand experience of the R.U. activities, the Foreign Secretary, Anthony Eden, accompanied by Lockhart, came to inspect the 'freedom stations' on June 25th 1942, although this coincided with quite a recent rumpus caused by the team at 'Dawn Edge', in Aspley Guise. When no one had been available to travel with them, they instead tended to make their own way to 'Simpsons', which now led to a strict reprimand that, in future, they must always be confined to the car en route 'and not be allowed to wander along the roads'!

Expanding the influence of P.W.E., consisting of David Bowes Lyon and Ritchie Calder, in March 1942, the first P.W.E. mission had been despatched to Washington and, in consequence, a group from the U.S. equivalent came to study methods of leaflet production. Then, on July 25th 1942, Harold Robin and Gambier Parry showed a party of Americans around 'Simpsons', demonstrating and explaining the broadcast recording facilities.

By the beginning of 1943, 23 stations were being broadcast, on disc, from four local transmitters, but on January 20th 1943, 'C', head of the Secret Service, sent for Lockhart and told him he would now take an option on all the P.W.E. buildings and staff. As a result, Brigadier Richard Gambier Parry, head of Secret Service Communications, would be retained on an agency basis, but for Air Commodore Blandy, who held joint responsibility for the supervision of P.W.E. communications, especially 'Aspidistra', there would be no position. 'Aspidistra', a powerful medium wave radio transmitter, linked to purpose built studios at Milton Bryan, was perhaps the most important of the P.W.E. broadcast projects and as such, together with Milton Bryan, is dealt with in a separate chapter. Also associated with Milton Bryan, as the inspiration of Sefton Delmer two important new broadcast stations – 'Atlantiksender' and 'Soldatensender Calais' – would begin transmission during the P.W.E. period and again their story is to be found in the relevant chapter.

In the early days of the propaganda broadcasts, all programmes had been recorded onto disc for transmission from the secret short wave radio stations. However, during the summer of 1941, heavy shipping losses in the Atlantic caused a severe shortage of records and for a while all R.U. transmissions were then made live which, as a matter of

The Rookery

In July 1942, recording equipment was installed, with an extension of the rehearsal apparatus to huts constructed in the garden. (J. Taylor, courtesy of the owner)

routine, only became possible following the construction of the Milton Bryan studio. Previously, the programmes had to be recorded at 'Simpsons', although, during July 1942, at 'The Rookery', Delmer's home in Aspley Guise, equipment was also installed for recording onto 12 inch discs, an extension of the rehearsal apparatus being made for huts in the garden. Often staying at the house, William Hottelot became the permanent Liaison Officer between the activities at 'The Rookery' and the U.S.A., and, also accommodated at the house, Miss Hodson joined the team in November 1942, as a new 'help'. Her duties would include accompanying the broadcast teams to Wavendon Towers.

THE TRAINING FOR P.W.E. OPERATIVES

Whenever new propaganda operations were planned, P.W.E. staff were 'ticketed', being formally cautioned by the security officer, the elderly Colonel Chambers and issued with a special card. No mention or discussion of the operation could then be made, except to someone able to produce a similar card.

In general the propagandists enjoyed no formal instruction, although personnel selected for fieldwork by P.W.E. and S.O.E. did undergo some degree of specialised training at a school near Woburn, run by Major John Hackett. On October 13th 1941, a propaganda training school had been first established at Pertenhall, 25 miles from Woburn, but this distance proved inconvenient and in a series of moves the centre was eventually re-located, in May 1942, to within six miles of C.H.Q. Here between four and ten agents attended at a time. In the autumn more staff were then employed and another move took place to a house in the near region of C.H.Q. The school had the benefit of a print shop, with assistance given by a P.W.E. compositor from Marylands.

The first officer trained for fieldwork in political warfare had been Lt. Colby, who, before sailing with the force tasked to occupy Madagascar, attended a two day course at C.H.Q. in March 1943. This proved useful experience for the French Region who, under the direction of Lt. Col. Sedgwick, then sent officers to C.H.Q. for around three weeks training in preparation for Operation Torch. A second course followed and Lt. Col. Sedgwick was duly appointed Commandant of the P.W.E. Training School, via a directive signed by the Director General on January 1st 1943.

The staff and students lived at Wing House, and included amongst the training were voice tests and actual broadcasts. The school was eventually scheduled for a move nearer London, but delays in securing the necessary domestic staff meant that further courses at C.H.Q., for officers chosen by the Joint Selection Board, were undertaken. These included that for nine British Commando officers in December 1943 and another in early 1944 for thirty two British and two American officers, (of which seventeen were Majors), on a Norwegian course.

Indeed, in anticipation of D Day, for their missions in the liberated countries and Germany, during 1943 and the relevant months of 1944 large numbers of 'political survey' officers, later to be known as 'propaganda intelligence officers', underwent training at the school, with S.O.E. maintaining communications through their radio network. Just before D Day, courses then began for a small number of British and American officers who, intending to link up with the local resistance, would be dropped behind enemy lines.

TOWARDS D DAY & BEYOND

With the preparations for D Day, despite the increasing magnitude of operational requirements, P.W.E. also had to attend domestic problems, and in May 1944, Bracken consulted with Lockhart about a P.W.E. burglary in the Woburn neighbourhood. However, since they lacked sufficient evidence, the police were unable to arrest the chauffeur suspected of the crime. Then, in another incident a P.W.E. housemaid gave birth to an illegitimate child by a local policeman. Arrangements were hurriedly made for the adoption of the child and the girl was bound over for two years, but P.W.E., as always, remained anonymous!

Yet, on the home scene, more serious disruptions were being caused by the beginning of the German V weapons campaign. During an alert all personnel at Bush House, London, were instructed to shelter in the bomb proof basement, but nevertheless, because of the inconvenience to their work, many staff ignored this directive. That is until a V1 skimmed the roof of the East Block and exploded in the Aldwych, wrecking the centre block and causing severe casualties. Most of the windows on the 6th, 7th and 8th floors of the North Wing were blown out and flying glass injured many of the staff.

Compounding the problems, following a second bout of eczema and prolonged treatment in the nursing homes of Edinburgh, the Director General, although back at work, was still not fully recovered. Moreover, the room at his London club had been bombed out and as an interim measure his chauffeur, McCoy, drove him to the Savoy before more permanent accommodation at a house near Radlett could be secured. Due to his infirmity, Lockhart had little option but to relax the responsibility of his duties, and he consequently asked the Governors of the B.B.C. to release Ivone Kirkpatrick as a Deputy Director General, with Major General Dallas Brooks responsible for the 'Country Establishment'.

Yet despite the high level upheavals, the work of the department had to go on and at C.H.Q., under the tightest security for a week prior to D Day, translators were kept busy translating the proclamations of Eisenhower into all the western languages. Two printing presses and their operators then also came under strict security for the production of the D Day leaflets, of which all but two would be produced by P.W.E., in conjunction with the American O.W.I.

Four days before the Invasion, Sefton Delmer now became Director of Special Operations and moved to London with official authority, on behalf of P.W.E., to negotiate with S.H.A.E.F. and other outside bodies. Assigned an office on the top floor of Bush House, together with his female personal assistant, he there received all manner of clandestine callers, who were in fact officers of the Underground Resistance groups, smuggled out of Occupied Europe. Delmer's task was to provide a part of the necessary briefing for their role in the coming Invasion.

V1 flying bomb

As emphasised by the damage caused to Bush House, the German V weapons posed a new threat to London. However, by the 'Double Cross' system, German agents under British control fed back false information, claiming that the bombs were overshooting the Capital. The Germans therefore lessened the range and many fell short in open countryside, on one occasion exploding on the perimeter of the aerodrome at Cranfield. (J. Taylor)

After the successful Normandy landings in June 1944, 'C', head of the Secret Service, requested the whole of Woburn Abbey and the associated accommodation 'for other purposes', but the onset of the German V2 campaign, targeted on London, instead meant that Woburn would be kept in reserve for P.W.E. Indeed, in view of the situation, on August 11th 1944 an emergency plan was approved by the Director General. By this it was proposed to accommodate one hundred and fifty three of the London personnel, plus chauffeurs and domestic staff, at Woburn with a provision for thirty more and, if necessary, a tented encampment could also house an additional one hundred. However, with the advance of the Allied armies in Europe, the threat from the V2s began to lessen while, with declining German morale, the propaganda began to have a telling effect. Even Goebbels had to admit; 'Enemy propaganda is beginning to have an uncomfortably noticeable effect on the German people. Anglo American leaflets are now no longer carelessly thrown aside but are read attentively; British broadcasts have a grateful audience'.

With the European war finally at an end in May 1945, discussions then began concerning arrangements for those people now leaving, or shortly to leave P.W.E. It was decided they would be given two months' pay in the form of a month's leave and a month's notice, and liquidation of the organisation began in June. On the grounds of ill health Lockhart resigned as Director General on August 1st 1945 and, before a dinner in private rooms of the Dorchester Hotel, on August 31st in the restaurant of Bush House he shook hands with some six hundred of the staff and took his final leave.

Most of the records of P.W.E. were deliberately destroyed at the end of the war, but, as perhaps an appropriate memento, at a subsequent furniture sale at 'The Rookery', Delmer's wartime headquarters, several scripts were then discovered in a small desk, written in German! Yet even after the end of the war, Aspley Guise continued to provide a haven for refugees and in 1956 a family of four Hungarians, fleeing from the Russians, came to live at a house in the village, for which the owner refused to take any rent. Made very welcome, they were relations of a Hungarian woman who had married a local builder, and arrived with the daughters wearing pyjamas under their siren suits, and the mother wearing a pair of her husband's trousers.

Dorchester Hotel

At the end of the war, P.W.E. was quickly disbanded and, as Director General, Robert Bruce Lockhart resigned on the grounds of ill health, on August 1st 1945. At the end of the month he then took his leave of the staff at Bush House, followed by a dinner in two private rooms of the Dorchester Hotel, in London. (The Wonderful Story of London)

CHAPTER SEVEN

MILTON BRYAN AND ASPIDISTRA

In August 1941, the Political Warfare Executive was given control of 'subversive' propaganda. However, for the radio broadcasts, except in exceptional circumstances only recorded transmissions were possible, but Sefton Delmer realised the impact that live broadcasts would have. When an ultra powerful radio transmitter, nicknamed 'Aspidistra', was bought from America and ultra modern studios were built at Milton Bryan, live broadcasts became routine and well justified his ambition.

Radio broadcasts had now become an established means of propaganda, but for the covert operations the existing facilities were limited to the recording studio at Wavendon Towers and therefore, except in exceptional circumstances, only the transmission of recorded programmes. Yet for the up to the minute thrust of contemporary news and personal stories, needed to give a novel edge, Sefton Delmer realised that live broadcasts were essential. Fortunately, in 1940 a combination of ambitions and circumstance then began a means to resolve the situation.

During one of his visits to Woburn Abbey, on learning of the insufficiency of the relatively low power shortwave transmitters at Potsgrove and Gawcott, Anthony Eden, the Foreign Secretary, became aware that an ultra powerful transmitter lay idle in America. Being too powerful for American use, the apparatus was about to be sold to the Chinese government, but Eden held immediate discussions with the head of the Special Operations Executive, Hugh Dalton, and in consequence Dalton sent a paper to the Prime Minister, Winston Churchill, explaining the merits. Churchill duly sanctioned the proposal in May 1941 and, as head of Secret Intelligence Service communications, Colonel Richard Gambier Parry then travelled to the U.S. to secure the option. He was shortly followed by the head of the technical side, Harold Robin, who, gaining familiarity with the equipment during the summer months, had travelled to America carrying the cheque for £523,000 – the purchase needing to be a commercial business transaction, since the United States had not yet entered the war, and could not be seen as covertly aiding Britain.

Built by R.C.A. for the WJ2 New Jersey commercial radio station, consisting of three 170KW units linked in series, though the apparatus had proved too powerful for American use, Robin suggested further improvements that increased the output by a fifth! The annual running costs were estimated at £28,000 and investigations now began towards the choosing of a suitable location. Initially a site near Woburn, in the disused quarry at Milton Bryan, had been favoured, convenient for the secret broadcast headquarters. However, this raised concern with the Air Ministry that the height of the aerial masts, plus their unusual strength, being made from high tensile steel instead of the usual tubes, might pose a hazard to aircraft operating from local training airfields. This, plus Harold Robin's reasoning that the transmitter should be as near to the enemy coast as possible, then caused a reconsideration. With the agreement of the newly created Political Warfare Executive, complete with a decoy installation a mile away, a 70 acre site in Ashdown Forest, near Crowborough, Sussex, became instead the preferred situation.

The need for an associated broadcast studio was now discussed, and on November 22nd 1941 a first meeting took place, a second meeting on the following day dealing with the layout and facilities. Proposals to accommodate the studio in Walton Rectory had to be dismissed, when the Admiralty made known they would retain the premises as overflow quarters for the Wrens working at Bletchley Park, although hopefully they remained unaware that the Rectory had been the scene of a recent suicide! Then on December 4th 1941, in a further meeting Colonel Gambier Parry suggested that a new building should be constructed. This view was duly reinforced on December 6th 1941, when Robin considered the existing possibilities of Potsgrove Rectory. On visiting the premises, he indeed found several attributes, including 'adequate water from a well', but the building lacked heat or power and matters were finally concluded when, two days later, Gambier Parry announced that the Rectory had been secured for the use of Fighter Command.

With Harold Robin's agreement, in the Canalletto Room at Woburn Abbey, attended by Gambier Parry, Harold Robin, Ralph Murray and Edward Halliday, discussions now took place regarding a new building for the studio, 'project 7850', and in consequence

Paris House

This print shows Paris House as the building appeared at the Paris Exhibition of 1878. The Duchess of Bedford had the building dismantled and shipped to England, to be rebuilt at Woburn. (Duke of Bedford)

Robin and Halliday began to investigate suitable locations. It was duly decided that the site should be in Woburn Park and, having examined the area, on December 8th 1941 they found a promising situation near to Paris House;

'Robin and E.H. examined ground in Park near Paris House for suitability for 'A' Studio site. The paddock next to the Bison enclosure is suitable for building (as is the Bison enclosure itself). The aerials to be alongside it with the U.H.F. hut on the higher ground next to Milton Bryant (visual for Dunstable Downs). This would bring the studios in proximity to Paris House, a possible dormitory for 'funnies'. Another possible site is inside the wall near the round reservoir, for both masts and studios with either a landline to the U.H.F. hut near M. Bryant or a tower of wood or steel to hold it at the required height. Robin says either of the above sites would do. The choice will depend on any difficulties that may arise over the "Ducal prejudices".'

Initially 'Maycrete' had been considered as a building material, but it was eventually concluded that, although at extra expense, brick would prove more suitable, especially for the walls of the broadcast studios. The proposal was duly considered and, another location having been dismissed near Eversholt which lacked seclusion and a south view, Colonel Gambier Parry was asked on December 11th 1941 to both requisition the site and prepare the necessary estimates.

Discussions having been held between Gambier Parry, Robin and the American engineers about the set up and control of the studio, on January 18th 1942, convened at 'Simpsons', as the codename for Wavendon Towers, on the next day an on site inspection took place. Then, on February 10th 1942, two men from the Woburn Estate, Wilson and Young, began digging the trial holes. Once inspected by the 'men from London', these were then immediately filled in, since the Estate Office had received a specific request that no cattle should be allowed in The Gravelpit Field until this had been done.

On February 17th 1942 the surveyors arrived to inspect the site and, on the chosen location, in a part of Mr. Lawson's Grange Farm, building duly began, the Thomas Bates Company of London and Coventry being engaged as the contractors. For a while, Mr. Lawson's son assumed the position of the firm's wages clerk, since the original employee had walked out of the job during the last month of the contract. Yet, in view of the tight security, he was never allowed to enter the main building.

Designed by Squadron Leader Edward Halliday, a trained architect, and incorporating a caretaker's flat, the building, of 'modernistic' appearance, resembled any of the many new factories now being erected around the country and included soundproofed studios, a large control room and a recreation room. Surrounded by a high chain

Squadron Leader Edward Halliday, the architect of the Milton Bryan studio. (Mr S. Halliday)

91

Milton Bryan guardhouse

The Milton Bryan studio was guarded by retired members of the local constabulary. Kennels for the Alsatian dogs were situated on the opposite side of the entrance road)Mr. S. Halliday)

Milton Bryan guardhouse – a present view. (J. Taylor)

link fence, surmounted by barbed wire, the premises stood within some five acres of grass, tarmac and tarred paths. From a specially-built guardhouse, uniformed special constables mounted a constant patrol with Alsatian dogs, the kennels being situated on the left of the entrance approach. On top of the guards' accommodation stood a water tank and, within the guardhouse, which included beds for off duty members, were secured rifles and tommy guns, regular firearms practice taking place in the grounds.

Also in the grounds was erected a forest of aerials, the wooden poles for which were especially carted in by a Leighton Buzzard firm. However, on one occasion work came to an unscheduled halt when one of the carts overturned! The elements could also pose a hazard, especially when a great gale blew down one of the lordly Cedar trees in the grounds of the village Manor House. (The tree had in fact been grown from a seed brought back from Mount Lebanon by the then Lord of the Manor, Sir Robert Inglis, in 1805.)

All the wiring and equipment for the studio were installed by personnel under the charge of Harold Robin and, apart from providing a small switchboard (immediately to the right upon entering the building, operated by three female G.P.O. telephonists from London), also laid on were high grade private lines. These linked the studio to the two wireless stations at Potsgrove and Gawcott, Aspidistra, Reuters, the Press Association and the prisoner of war interrogation centres at Latimer and Wilton Park. With the building work now complete, the construction company then left, to begin a new contract for the airfield at Thetford, in Norfolk.

Professional G.P.O. telephonists, from London exchanges such as that shown above, were recruited for duties at the Milton Bryan studio. (The Wonderful Story of London)

Amongst the several ancillary buildings associated with the studio, situated directly opposite stood two air raid shelters, and they proved their subsequent worth late one night when probing the skies above Woburn Abbey, an enemy aircraft suddenly dropped several incendiaries and then returned to deliver two high explosive bombs. Cottages at nearby Battlesden suffered a near miss but, had the bombs been dropped a couple of seconds later, the Milton Bryan studio would definitely have been hit. At Potsgrove there was another 'bomb' scare when the wife of a labourer found a hessian package hidden in the barn. She feared it might be a bomb left by parachutists, but in fact it turned out to be a quantity of cement, filched from the builders by her husband!

Pronouncing the Milton Bryan studio 'very fine' and the police gatehouse as 'almost

93

palatial', on Monday, 19th October 1942, the Director General of the Political Warfare Executive, Robert Bruce Lockhart, officially inspected the premises with Colonel Cole, the Home Office Inspector and Commander Willis, the Chief Constable. Now the required facilities for live broadcasting – with the most powerful transmitter in Europe – were finally ready and, as recounted in the appropriate chapter, this potential Sefton Delmer would exploit to the full.

Delmer had been the obvious choice for Milton Bryan but, although the studio may have been nearing an operational use, even by August 1942 any decision regarding the use of Aspidistra was still lacking. Having originally sanctioned the purchase of the transmitter, Winston Churchill now became involved and the following month demanded to know when transmissions would start; 'First explain what advantages it gives us (8 lines), secondly report every three days the day it is expected to be ready to function'. Three days later Lockhart reported that one part was being flown in from America, although he 'omitted' to mention that only one of the three masts had yet been erected! (On a technical note, the three masts would be erected in a triangular configuration, which, by varying the signal strengths, then allowed a measure of directional propagation). As an added delay, a ship carrying one of the masts had been torpedoed in the Atlantic.

On September 23rd 1942, Lockhart then reported that the second mast was a third complete and the third mast was on its way from the docks. However, he had to reveal that reserve equipment was not available, to which Churchill tersely replied; 'Have we really built this gigantic machine dependent on valves which are obsolete with no

Milton Bryan personnel

With the Milton Bryan studio in the background, amongst this group of people Squadron Leader Edward Halliday stands on the left. An architect and talented artist, he designed the building at Milton Bryan and was responsible for the day-to-day administration. Harold Robin, head of the technical side of the Secret Intelligence Service communications, is third from the left. (Mr. S. Halliday)

provision for replacement?' Some new and used valves were then hurriedly procured! Lockhart now gave the date of October 15th 1942 for the first operation and during that month the first full power tests were indeed conducted, although with rather dramatic results when the omission of an earthing pin caused a live arc! Following tests from receptive areas, connected by a direct line to Milton Bryan, at last the three masted installation lay ready. (Later in the war all three masts were nearly lost when a V1 flying bomb passed between them!) Not only did Lockhart eventually succeed in acquiring the exclusive use but he also ensured that only S.I.S. engineers were employed for the operation and not those of the B.B.C.

The first transmission on Aspidistra was made on November 9th 1942, concerning the landings in North Africa. In fact this was a special message from President Roosevelt to the French, and had been recorded by Roosevelt's nephew in the Oval Office of the White House onto a 6 inch disc. This was then especially flown to Britain and delivered to Wavendon Towers, where it was copied for broadcast onto a larger, standard disc.

'Get off my Aspidistra!'

For special duties in connection with Aspidistra, the high power radio transmitter, Air Commodore Blandy was seconded to P.W.E. However, as head of S.I.S. communications Brigadier Gambier Parry did much to thwart his active involvement and, in this sketch by Squadron Leader Halliday, Harold Robin also displays a certain bias by telling him to 'get off my Aspidistra!' (Mr. S. Halliday)

By the arrangement of Lockhart, as the Director General, on February 5th 1943, Sefton Delmer took charge of the Milton Bryan premises with his deputy Karl Robson, a Major from the War Office (formerly a pre-war newspaper correspondent in Berlin). Seconded to P.W.E., for special duties, in connection with Aspidistra, Air Commodore Lyster Blandy was also appointed, since the R.A.F. signals section expressed an interest in the use. Earlier in the war, Blandy had been tasked to establish Special Air Intelligence Section A11(e), created to intercept and exploit the lax wireless security of German aircrews, and by his P.W.E. duties he was now supposed to supervise the technical control and security of Aspidistra. Yet Gambier Parry, by now a Brigadier, did much to thwart his active involvement, refusing to authorise his visits to the transmitter and failing to notify him of the test transmissions. Nevertheless, Blandy provided valuable wireless advice to the department.

Supported by the evidence of aerial photographs, rushed to Milton Bryan by despatch rider, M.B., as the codename for the centre, soon became acclaimed for high grade intelligence, gathering information from a multitude of sources. From the debrief of R.A.F. crews, regular reports revealed the damage caused by bombing raids. As a further input, a direct landline connected the centre with the Combined

Bomb damage

Milton Bryan gained increasing renown as a centre for the gathering and analysis of high grade intelligence. Information came from a variety of sources, including aerial photographs of bomb damage, rushed to the Studio by motorcycle despatch rider. (Britain's Wonderful Air Force)

Services Detailed Interrogation Centre and on the upper level of the building 24 hour monitoring of enemy radio transmissions was maintained, any information of interest being captured on wire recorders. These were the forerunners of tape recorders but for Hugh Gaitskell, who had been deeply involved with the propaganda activities, during the period when Hugh Dalton had been in charge, the existence of such machines long seemed a mystery for, when being interviewed as leader of the Labour party in 1961, he remarked of the 'bulky Grundig', being used to record the occasion, 'What a remarkable machine – how does it work?'!

As the chief intelligence expert, Clifton Child, a young education officer from Manchester, had the task of examining all this information, and also recruited was C. Stevens, an Oxford Ancient History don, and Max Braun. Assisted by a team of graduate girl researchers, the group soon evolved into an exceptional intelligence department and indeed, within a select circle the reputation of Milton Bryan gained increasing renown. Many high ranking British and American personnel arrived to inspect the newspaper and radio newsrooms, intelligence files, studios and extensive record library. Conducted by Henry Zeisel, even records were especially made at Milton Bryan by the German equivalent of the E.N.S.A. band, which had been captured in North Africa by the Eighth Army. Further, providing music of the required 'flavour', at the Albert Hall the band of the Royal Marines also recorded for Milton Bryan, and in America Marlene Dietrich made special records, although unaware of their purpose. The musical content certainly captured the attention of the audience and even Himmler acknowledged that 'we have forbidden listening in to enemy stations, but we have not been able to punish all who have listened'.

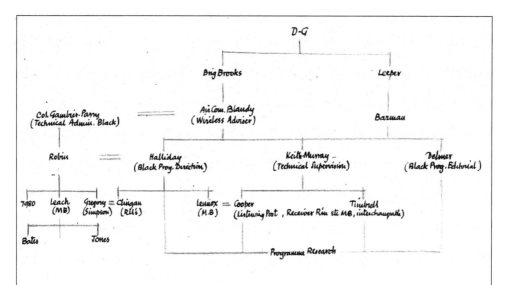

In this 'family tree' of the operational set up, 'D-G' refers to the Director General, Sir Robert Bruce Lockhart. 'M.B.' is the code for Milton Bryan and the function of key personnel is given. Air Commodore Blandy, seconded to P.W.E. for special duties in connection with 'Aspidistra', is depicted as liaising with Colonel Gambier Parry, although the arrangement was rather one-sided! (Mr. I. Murray)

By May 1943 Delmer had been promoted to Director of Special Operations against the Enemy and Satellites, and accordingly the heads and servicing personnel of all the Enemy and Satellite R.U.s were transferred to the Milton Bryan compound. Hastily erected, prefabricated barracks now accommodated the necessary intelligence teams, with editorial writers, secretaries and speakers employed to deal with Italy, Hungary, Bulgaria and Romania. In fact so many R.U.s were now in operation that literally tons of recording discs were being produced. Supposedly these were destroyed after use, but in reality were brought to Milton Bryan, for covert storage!

With a committee appointed by Reginald Leeper, as the head of SO1, since the spring of 1942 discussions on the best employment of Aspidistra had continued at C.H.Q. (Woburn Abbey) and it would not be long before a very important use was found. P.W.E. experts had realised that certain German medium wave musical transmissions contained a secret code for communicating with night fighters. When this was proved, as programme manager, Squadron Leader Halliday then suggested that Aspidistra could be used to jam these transmissions, and this measure subsequently proved extremely successful. As a refinement, it was then suggested that 'Soldatensender Calais' (Soldiers Radio Calais) could also be just as effective, and consequently, when required, this would be transmitted on the enemy wavelength.

At Milton Bryan, a routine day would find Delmer beginning his duties around 9.30a.m., reading the latest batch of Foreign Office telegrams and S.I.S. reports in his office. At 10.45a.m. an editorial conference would then be convened in the central operations room and this would last until approximately 2p.m. The afternoon was taken up by the writing of talks and news preparation. Amongst the chief newswriters

Albrechet Ernst had made Delmer's acquaintance during the Spanish Civil War, and also included was Hans Gutmann, a prewar art dealer in Berlin, and Dr. Albert, formerly a press attache of the Austrian Legation who, when Hitler came to power, wisely remained in Britain. As the chief 'disc jockey', Alex Maas, a broadcaster, had also known Delmer during the Spanish Civil War and, at Delmer's request, on fleeing Germany en route for Mexico, he and his wife had been intercepted by the Secret Service in Bermuda.

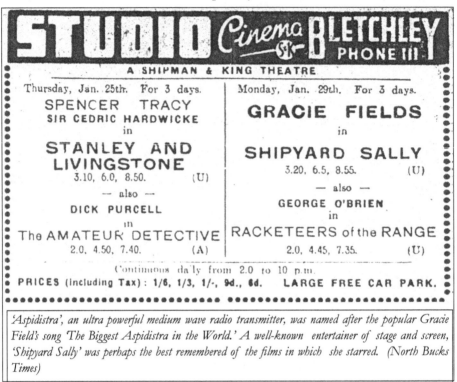

STUDIO Cinema **BLETCHLEY**
PHONE III

A SHIPMAN & KING THEATRE

Thursday, Jan. 25th. For 3 days.	Monday, Jan. 29th. For 3 days.
SPENCER TRACY SIR CEDRIC HARDWICKE in	GRACIE FIELDS in
STANLEY AND LIVINGSTONE 3.10, 6.0, 8.50. (U)	SHIPYARD SALLY 3.20, 6.5, 8.55. (U)
— also —	— also —
DICK PURCELL in	GEORGE O'BRIEN in
The AMATEUR DETECTIVE 2.0, 4.50, 7.40. (A)	RACKETEERS of the RANGE 2.0, 4.45, 7.35. (U)

Continuous daily from 2.0 to 10 p.m.

PRICES (including Tax): 1/6, 1/3, 1/-, 9d., 6d.   LARGE FREE CAR PARK.

'Aspidistra', an ultra powerful medium wave radio transmitter, was named after the popular Gracie Field's song 'The Biggest Aspidistra in the World.' A well-known entertainer of stage and screen, 'Shipyard Sally' was perhaps the best remembered of the films in which she starred. (North Bucks Times)

By the end of 1943, Milton Bryan had begun using Aspidistra to wreak havoc with German air force operations, assisted by several captured personnel with recent experience of the genuine Luftwaffe. The deception involved recording German ground control instructions on one night and then re-transmitting them to the night fighters on the next, thereby sending the German aircraft on all manner of false interceptions. Another plan involved co-operation with the R.A.F. As their bombers headed towards a German city, to avoid becoming a homing beacon the local radio station would then go off the air. Devised by Harold Robin, by means of an electronic switch holding off the Aspidistra carrier wave, when this happened an 'alternative' broadcast from Milton Bryan would immediately transmit on the same frequency. With presenters at Milton Bryan mimicking the original German announcers, the actual delay, of about 6 milliseconds, proved imperceptible to the listening audience, and with the station now 'taken over' and the audience none the wiser, all manner of false instructions could be given! On one occasion, whilst monitoring such a station, Delmer demanded to know why Milton Bryan had not come on the air. He was then informed that it had and he was in fact listening to studio announcers sitting not many yards from his own office!

By March 1944, around a hundred 'collaborators', including some forty Germans, were now under Delmer's control at Milton Bryan, bussed in daily from dormitories to include 'The Holt' and 'Dawn Edge', in Aspley Guise. Therefore, it was perhaps fortunate that the studio enjoyed a secluded situation, since many of the personnel pursued a novel form of relaxation, sunbathing nude on the roof!

By now plans were being prepared for the Invasion of Europe, and for his consequent role Delmer was assigned an office on the top floor of the P.W.E. headquarters in London, at Bush House. Soon he was appointed Director of Special Operations and in round the clock broadcasts attempted now to confuse the enemy as to where the actual landings would take place. One rumour suggested that only those army units deemed smart and efficient were being sent to the Russian Front, thereby hoping to encourage sloppiness in those divisions within the Invasion area. Yet perhaps not grasping the importance of these measures, at this crucial time Brendan Bracken seemed quite willing to hand over Aspidistra to the Americans for a forces entertainment programme. Thankfully, sanity prevailed!

As a further preparation to the build up, Delmer now conceived the idea of a German newspaper, 'Nachrichten für die Truppe' (News for the Troops) to be produced at Milton Bryan and dropped from the air over enemy troop concentrations. With a certain amount of disinformation, the paper would otherwise bring factual news denied to the German troops by their own authorities and so help towards a general demoralisation. As an Anglo American venture, the staff for the newspaper worked in hastily erected pre-fab huts in the Milton Bryan compound, and on D Day, 6th June, M.B. intercepted a newsflash concerning the Invasion, transmitted by the German news agency. The front page of 'Nachrichten' was then quickly changed to promote the D Day story!

On July 20th 1944, in the aftermath of the Invasion, the Milton Bryan newsroom then intercepted details of a bomb plot against Hitler, and immediately the intelligence teams began to implicate as many of the German Werhmacht as possible! In fact Milton Bryan would soon become acquainted with the only member of the 'Generals Conspiracy'

Inside the Milton Bryan Studio

When built, Milton Bryan contained the very latest in state of the art technology. The equipment has long since been removed but several features still remain, to include sound proofing tiles and electrical fittings. (David & Debra Rixon)

Sketches of Milton Bryan personnel. The architect of the Milton Bryan studio, Squadron Leader Edward Halliday, was a talented artist who made several sketches of the personnel involved in the daily duties. In an old tin trunk, unopened since the end of the war, his son, Stephen, recently discovered a treasure trove of documents relating to the wartime work at Milton Bryan – including this collection of untitled sketches! (Mr. S. Halliday)

101

to escape abroad, Otto John. After several adventures he was flown from Lisbon to Poole by the Secret Service and conveyed to the Chelsea Oratory, London, a centre for the screening of foreign nationals. In due course he was interviewed by Delmer, 'a corpulent gentleman in mufti', about the possibility of working for British propaganda, and in December 1944 was issued with an I.D. card in the name of 'Oskar Jurgens'. In a military car he was told he was being taken to 'a house in the country' and arriving in the evening 'At the great gates of a park full of ancient trees' eventually came to a guardroom, where uniformed men could be seen carrying sub machine guns. A policeman identified the woman driver and after a few dozen yards the car stopped in front of 'a hermetically blacked-out building'.

Otto was led into the building, along a corridor and to a door, above which glowed a red light. He then entered alone to find Delmer seated behind a large desk, on which was scattered an array of papers, telephones and Dictaphones. After signing a pledge of secrecy, Otto now learned that he was standing in the offices of 'Soldatensender' and would be told more about the organisation the following morning. Meanwhile, taken to 'The Rookery', he there had the chance to meet some of the other 'black' propagandists. Not being allowed, by a British directive, to broadcast, he became an assistant to Clifton Child and helped to sift and evaluate the incoming intelligence. Otherwise he spent

The Hitler Bomb Plot

In the aftermath of the D Day landings, a group of German generals seized the opportunity to assassinate Hitler. A bomb was planted whilst Hitler was attending a meeting at the 'Wolf's Lair', at Rastenburg, in East Prussia, but, although exploding, left the Fuhrer still alive. Many were to perish in the purge that followed. After several adventures, aided by the British Secret Service the only member of the 'Generals Conspiracy' to escape abroad was eventually brought to Milton Bryan. (Sunday Express)

Kehlsteinhaus The Eagles Nest

Towards the end of the war, the Special Operations Executive planned a commando raid on Hitler's mountain headquarters, intending to assassinate Hitler and Himmler. In the event the raid was called off, but at Milton Bryan the vast amounts of information gained during the planning were put to good use. (War Illustrated)

103

his days exploring the station and familiarising himself with the files, which proved an extremely useful exercise, for S.O.E. had devised a plan to launch a commando raid on Hitler's mountain headquarters, intending to assassinate not only him but also Himmler. However, in the event the attack was called off, but the vast amounts of intelligence amassed in the preparation were directed to Milton Bryan and subsequently used in news reports. These proved so accurate that Hitler became convinced there must be spies at his H.Q.!

Causing further distress to the Germans by the selective 'hijack' of German radio stations, Milton Bryan announcers, via Aspidistra, began to broadcast all manner of false instructions, designed to cause congestion and panic as the Reich collapsed. Indeed, the ruse proved so successful that even Allied authorities were deceived and the Joint Intelligence Committee had to be informed, lest it believed the information was genuine!

Towards the close of 1944 the end of the war seemed nigh and after the fall of Calais, in August 1944, 'Soldatensender Calais' became renamed 'Soldatensender West', transmitting the final broadcast on April 14th 1945. Shaving off his beard, Delmer then threw a party in the Milton Bryan canteen and for the first time staff from different locations were allowed to socialise. Delmer and a section of his staff now prepared themselves for new duties and, moving to London, would make arrangements to reconstruct the press and radio in the British Occupied Zone.

Whilst the facilities at Milton Bryan were no longer needed for propaganda broadcasts, the recording equipment still had one more important role to play. Having been instrumental in the code breaking activities at Bletchley Park, during the later months of the war Alan Turing had been developing a secure speech encipherment system at Hanslope Park. Codenamed 'Delilah' (the deceiver of men), by the spring of 1945 the system was ready for test, and this was then arranged at the Milton Bryan studios. A demonstration was recorded onto a 16 inch disc, but during the proceedings Alan's braces burst, and as a temporary remedy Harold Robin produced some bright red cord from an American packing case. Alan, however, used this as a permanent substitute for his braces thereafter!

The propaganda activities at Milton Bryan were finally at an end, and in due course the Post Office arrived to collect the multitude of now surplus telephones. For a while the premises became a hostel for displaced persons, and later there were plans to use the building for light industrial use. Restrictions caused by the local green belt policy prevented this from going ahead, however, and the building became derelict. The boiler house, annexed to the main building, was recently demolished due to the amounts of asbestos, but certain of the other outbuildings still remain. Presently the site is held under lease by the Scout Association, as a camping area for the Ampthill and Woburn District.

On September 4th 2002, to recognise the achievements of the wartime personnel, a commemorative plaque was unveiled at the studio by Lord Howland, now the Duke of Bedford, of Woburn Abbey. Arranged by John Taylor, funding had been kindly provided by the Bedfordshire Tourist Board and Emerson Valley Combined School, Milton Keynes.

The unveiling ceremony of the Commemorative Plaque at the Milton Bryan Studio, on September 4th, 2002
Left: from left to right. The Duke of Bedford (then Lord Howland), Ingram Murray, John Taylor.
Right: The scene at the ceremony including authentic vehicles and – kindly arranged by the local Scouts Association – a N.A.A.F.I. tent. (Photos courtesy of David and Debra Rixon)

Nr. 327, Freitag, 9. März 1945

NACHRICHTEN FÜR DIE TRUPPE

Eisenhower geht über den Rhein

Starke USA-Kräfte fassen auf dem rechten Ufer Fuss

DER schwerste Schlag gegen die Verteidigung des Reiches im Westen seit der Landung der Alliierten in der Normandie ist jetzt am Rhein zwischen Bonn und Koblenz geführt worden.

Starke Verbände amerikanischer Truppen haben bei Remagen den Rhein überschritten und führen ihrem Brückenkopf, nach letzten Meldungen, laufend Verstärkungen an Truppen und Material zu.

Der amerikanische Vorstoss über den Rhein hat alle Berechnungen der Führung über den Haufen geworfen.

Im Hauptquartier des Ob. West hatte man eine Überquerung des Rheins südlich Köln für undurchführbar gehalten. Die Leichtigkeit, mit der die Amerikaner bei Remagen den Rhein mit starken Kräften überschreiten konnten, zwingt die Führung, jetzt auch mit weiteren alliierten Vorstössen über den Rhein an anderen Abschnitten zu rechnen.

Die ersten Amerikaner fassten schon Dienstag nachmittag, etwa um 16 Uhr 30, Fuss auf dem rechten Rheinufer, nur kurz nachdem starke amerikanische Verbände im Ahrtal bis nach Remagen durchgebrochen waren.

Überraschung

Die Rheinüberquerung kam so unerwartet, dass nichts da war, um den Amerikanern die Landung am rechten Ufer streitig zu machen. Noch in den Abendstunden und gestern im Laufe des Tages setzten die Amerikaner immer mehr Truppen über den Rhein. In aller Eile zusammengezogene Alarmverbände konnten nichts gegen die amerikanischen Sturmeinheiten ausrichten.

Grosse Panzerbereitstellungen bei Erpel auf dem rechten Rheinufer fielen den Amerikanern fast kampflos in die Hand. Kein Tropfen Sprit war

(Fortsetzung Seite 4)

Ring um Danzig und Gotenhafen immer enger

Von Hinterpommern, wo nur noch aufgesplitterte Verbände der Heeresgruppe Mitte der Vernichtung zu entgehen suchen, und von Westpreussen, wo gestern Berent und Bütow gefallen sind und der Ring um Danzig und Gotenhafen jede Stunde enger wird, hat sich das Schwergewicht der Kämpfe jetzt an die Oderfront vor Berlin verschoben.

Immer mehr Sowjetverstärkungen greifen in den Kampf um die Ausgangsstellungen für den Grossangriff auf Berlin ein. Der Brückenkopf auf dem Westufer der Oder südwestlich Küstrin ist in den letzten 36 Stunden erheblich grösser geworden. Bis in den Raum von Seelow, 20 km westlich Küstrin, waren Sowjettruppen bereits vorgestossen, ehe sie durch einen Flankenangriff der deutschen Truppen gestoppt und zurückgeworfen wurden.

Alles was an Reserven verfügbar ist wird zu Gegenangriffen eingesetzt, um die Sowjetvorstösse aufzufangen. Dabei haben einige ganze Reihe von Ortschaften schon wiederholt den Besitzer gewechselt. Besonders erbittert sind die Kämpfe um die Trümmer von Rathstock und Manschnow.

Die deutsche Besatzung in Küstrin hat bisher allen Angriffen auf die Festungswerke standgehalten. Alles wird getan, um die Verteidigung von Küstrin zu stärken, da die Sowjets erst dann zu dem entscheidenden Stoss auf Berlin antreten können, wenn sie die Festung Küstrin aus der Abwehrfront vor Berlin herausgebrochen haben.

Auf breiter Front

Der bedeutendste Rückschlag der von den übrigen Abschnitten der Ostfront gemeldet wird, traf die eingekesselten Truppen im Kessel Danzig - Gotenhafen, wo Sowjettruppen die Verkehrsknotenpunkte Berent und Bütow genommen haben und jetzt auf breiter Front weiter nach Norden vordringen.

Auch die Stadt Schlawe in Hinterpommern ging verloren. Rund 2 000 Mann stellten in diesem Abschnitt den Kampf ein und gaben sich gefangen.

Zugleich ist Danzig jetzt auch stärker von Osten bedroht

(Fortsetzung Seite 4)

Zwei, die noch an den Sieg glauben

MUTSCHMANN · LOHSE

Eine eindrucksvolle Demonstration unbedingter Siegeszuversicht gab Gauleiter Mutschmann am Vorabend seines 66. Geburtstags. Auf einem Betriebsappell in Zwickau erklärte Pg. Mutschmann:

„Genau wie 1918 haben wir auch heute wieder den sicheren Sieg in der Tasche. Aber damals wurde uns der Sieg durch die Umgebung des Kaisers, die nich al es auf den Sieg gesetzt hatte in den letzten

Niemand lässt sich von den schweren Schlägen, die die deutsche Abwehr im Osten und Westen seit Wochen erleidet, weniger einschüchtern, als von seinem Posten als Reichskommissar Ostland vertriebene Gauleiter Hinrich Lohse. Auf einer Kreistagung, die kürzlich in Segeberg, Gau Schleswig-Holstein stattfand, rief Gauleiter Lohse aus:

„Je schwerer die Not heute ist und je grösser die Sorgen sind, desto nationalsozia...

Im Westen:

Flucht nach dem Süden

Nach dem schnellen Vorstoss des Feindes zum Rhein bis hinauf nach Koblenz und der überraschenden Bildung eines Brückenkopfes auf dem rechten Rheinufer verlassen jetzt Tausende von Flüchtlingen ihre Wohnungen in der Nähe des Rheinufers, um nicht von der Schlacht um weitere Rheinübergänge überrascht zu werden. Wer irgend kann, versucht sich nach Süddeutschland durchzuschlagen, wo die Versorgungslage noch immer am besten ist.

Güterwagen mit Lebensmitteln, Flakgeschützen und Flakmunition für Süddeutschland geniessen auf Anordnung der Parteikanzlei Vorrang vor allen anderen Eisenbahntransporten, nachdem jetzt in Süddeutschland eine grössere Zahl von Amtsträgern und Beamten der Partei lebt als je zuvor.

Im Osten:

Sowjetpanzer beobachten—!

Jeder Zivilist in der Mark Brandenburg, in Pommern, Sachsen und anderen frontnahen Gebieten wurde gestern durch Rundfunk und Presse aufgefordert, alliierte Bewegungen zu beobachten und zu melden, um der Wehrmacht „im Kampf gegen den Einbruch der „östischen Steppe" zu helfen.

Jeder einzelne soll mithelfen, da die Wehrmacht allein heute nicht mehr in der Lage, die Bekämpfung von durchgebrochenen Sowjet...

---

1 002 579 ergaben sich im Westen

Seit der Invasion haben 1 002 579 Wehrmachtangehörige im Westen den Kampf eingestellt und sich gefangen gegeben.

Diese Ziffer entspricht dem Mannschaftsbestand von 100 kampfstarken Divisionen.

Rund 140 000 Mann haben auf deutschem Boden Schluss gemacht.

CHAPTER EIGHT

NACHRICHTEN FÜR DIE TRUPPE

Apart from the radio broadcasts, printed propaganda was also devised at Milton Bryan, and in the preparations for D Day a newspaper for the German troops was produced. Dropped by air, this proved so popular, through the content of factual news, sports coverage and even pin ups, that the German authorities tried unsuccessfully to prevent the paper from being read by their soldiers.

In the preparations for the D Day landings, following a communication to Major General Brooks on February 15th 1944, as the inspiration of Sefton Delmer 'Nachrichten für die Truppe', (News for the Troops), was proposed as a daily newspaper destined for the German army. An alternative to the heavily censored offerings from their own authorities, the paper would provide factual, up to date news, coupled with sports results and glamour pin ups, and to maintain the interest no political slants or preachings would be employed.

The operation began in early March 1944 and, as an Anglo American venture, through the efforts of John Elliot, advertising agencies, newspaper, magazine and broadcast agencies across America supplied the suitable talent. Working from pre-fabricated huts in the grounds of the Milton Bryan studio, the personnel came under the direction of Delmer and, as an inspiration to the staff, he supervised the editorial control and wrote much of the material. Every night this then formed the content of the paper, accompanied by information edited and rewritten from the news and talks of the 'Soldatensender' radio programme.

At Milton Bryan the paper would be written during the early morning and before 11am the layout, embellished with illustrations and photographs under the supervision of Harold Keeble, was then finalised at the P.W.E. print facility at 'Marylands', near Woburn. In April, after several attempts, a test issue was duly produced for printing by the Luton News (Home Counties Newspapers) in Alma Street, Luton, and this would be in addition to their usual six local newspapers.

Consisting of two 13 inch by 9 inch pages, April 25th saw the first edition of 300,000 copies ready for the next stage of delivery but, despite this being the first issue, it was actually printed as being no. 11 to confuse the German authorities! Tied into manageable bales on the publishing bench, these were then transported to an associated Luton firm, Gibbs and Bamforth. (After the war this became the Leagrave Press). 'Knocked up' by female employees, two guillotines then respectively cut off the fold and separated the resulting two copies.

The workforce was apparently sustained by a supply of cheese rolls from Mrs. Ritson's canteen and, in view of the prevailing security, very few additional staff were employed for the operation. Work continued 7 days a week and no leave could be taken. John Gibbs, assisted by his brother Richard, the joint managing director of the firm, then helped pack the copies – together with forged ration books and leave passes

NEWS FOR THE TROOPS

Eisenhower crosses the Rhine

Powerful US forces gain a foothold on the right bank of the river

The heaviest blow against the defence of the realm in the west, since the Allied Forces landed in Normandy, has now been dealt between Bonn and Koblenz.

According to latest reports, powerful units of American troops have crossed the Rhine at Remagen, and support their bridgehead by channelling a constant flow of reinforcements of men and supplies towards it.

The American advance across the Rhine has thrown all strategic planning by the military high command into complete disarray.

At the headquarters of the High Command West a crossing of the Rhine south of Cologne had been deemed impossible. The ease with which the Americans were able to cross the Rhine at Remagen using a strong contingent of men, compels the military leadership to anticipate further enemy advances across the Rhine along other sections of the river.

As early as Tuesday afternoon, at around 16.30 p.m., the first Americans gained a foothold on the right hand bank of the Rhine, shortly after powerful units had broken through to Remagen from the Ahr- valley.

Surprise

The Rhine crossing was so unexpected, that there was nothing to stop them from landing on the other side. Still on the same night and yesterday during the day the Americans transferred more and more troops across the Rhine. Emergency units quickly assembled in last minute haste were powerless against the American special attack landing units. Extensive lines of tank defences near Erpel on the right bank of the Rhine fell to the Americans almost without any resistance. Not even a drop of fuel was

(Continued on Page 4)

1,002,579 Surrendered in the West

Since the invasion, 1,002,579 German soldiers have stopped fighting on the western front and have surrendered as prisoners of war. This figure corresponds to the equivalent manpower of 100 fighting divisions.

Around 140,000 men have given themselves up on German territory.

In the West

Escape towards the South

Following the speedy enemy breakthrough to the Rhine right up to Coblenz, and the unexpected establishment of an enemy bridgehead on the right hand bank of the Rhine, thousands are now fleeing their homes near the river to avoid getting caught up in the fighting for further Rhine crossings.

Whoever is able to, tries to make his way through to Southern Germany where the supply situation is still by far the best.

Goods trains packed with food, anti-aircraft guns and anti-aircraft ammunition bound for Southern Germany are now given preferential treatment ahead of all other rail transport under orders from the Reichs-Chancellery. This is due to the fact that a larger number of party bosses and civil servants have now retreated to Southern Germany.

In the East

Watch out for Soviet Tanks!

Radio and press have appealed to every citizen in Mark Brandenburg, Pomerania, Saxony and other areas close to the front lines to monitor and report Allied troop movements, in order to help the German army in the fight against the collapse of the Eastern Steppes.

Every single man is needed as the army alone is no longer able to keep up the fight against Soviet tanks which have penetrated the front lines.

Enemy tightens its Stranglehold on Danzig and Gotenhafen

The centre of the battle has now shifted to the banks of the river Oder just outside Berlin — away from Eastern Pomerania where only a few remaining splinter groups of the central army are now trying to evade certain extinction, and also away from Western Prussia where Bütow and Berent have fallen to the enemy, and where the enemy stranglehold on Danzig and Gotenhafen gets tighter by the hour.

More and more Soviet reinforcements are joining the battle for key positions for the main attack on Berlin. The bridgehead on the western bank of the Oder south of Küstrin has considerably grown in size during the last 36 hours.

Soviet troops had already advanced to the area around Seelow, 20 km west of Küstrin, before being stopped and pushed back by a German counter attack.

Anything available in terms of reserves is being used for counter attacks to bring the Soviet advance to a halt. In the course of the fighting a whole range of places have changed hands several times. Particularly bitter fighting is continuing for the ruins of Rathstock and Marischnow. German defending forces in Küstrin have so far withstood all attacks on the fortifications of the town. Everthing is done to reinforce the defence of Küstrin because the Soviets can only begin their decisive breakthrough towards Berlin, once the fortified town has been cut off from the rest of the German defence lines.

Along a broad front

The most significant setback being reported by other sections on the eastern front was suffered by encircled troops in the stranglehold of Danzig — Gotenhafen, as Soviet troops have occupied Berent and Bütow, where vital supply routes meet. They are now pushing north along a broad front.

The town Schlave in Eastern Pomerania also fell to the enemy. Around 2000 men in this area gave up their weapons and surrendered. At the same time Danzig is now under increased attack from the east

(Continued page 4)

Two who still believe in victory

MUTSCHMANN

Regional section leader (Gauleiter) Mutschmann gave an impressive demonstration of unconditional belief in victory on the eve of his 66th birthday. During a rousing speech at a factory in Zwickau Pg. Mutschmann declared:

Just as in 1918, we are again assured certain victory. But in those days we were robbed of our victory in the last minute by powerful forces surrounding the empeiur who had not risked everything for victory.

LOHSE

No one other than Gauleiter Hinrich Lohse, driven from his post of Reichs-commissioner in charge of the eastern provinces, could feel less intimidated by the heavy setbacks suffered by German defences in the east and in the west during the past few weeks. At a regional council meeting in Bad Segeberg, Schleswig-Holstein, he proclaimed:

The heavier the burden and hardship is today, and the greater our worries, the more national socialist will our future be one day.

– into leaflet bombs, supplied by the American Air Force. These had to be ready by 5p.m. for collection by lorries of the American Night Leaflet Squadron, and a single codeword, giving the departure time for the day, was then telephoned to the airfield at Cheddington, to confirm that the vehicles were en route. At Cheddington the bombs were then loaded onto the B17s of the 422nd Squadron, U.S.A.A.F., for delivery that night.

The squadron had arrived in England during 1942 as a regular bomber unit of the 305th Group, but from April 1944 began to work with Delmer's unit as the Special Leaflet Squadron, being exclusively assigned to this role in October 1943. By December 1944, the R.A.F. also began using the leaflet bomb, with aircraft of No. 1, 3 and 5 Groups assisting in the task.

When the weather conditions initially postponed the launch of D Day, the redundant copies of the 'Nachrichten' issue, which had already been loaded into 100 leaflet bombs, were hurriedly collected for destruction by the Americans. In fact, for reasons of security, they routinely disposed of any waste paper that collected around the rotary print equipment.

On June 6th 1944 the German news agency then put out an urgent newsflash concerning the Invasion and, intercepted by the Hellschreiber at Milton Bryan and embellished with a little more 'information', a subsequent broadcast was soon transmitted on 'Soldatensender'. Delmer drove hurriedly to Marylands for the new front page of 'Nachrichten', and that day production peaked at one million copies. Locked into the factory, to ensure that not a word could be said to anyone outside the building, the process workers had arrived at 3.30am and by 10am they were running off the story of D Day with full details.

Prior to the Invasion, the paper had been routinely dropped over Holland, Belgium, Norway and Denmark as well as France, and it was thereby hoped to confuse the enemy as to where the landings might be expected. Exempt from unneccesary censorship, additional information for 'Nachricten' was supplied from the operations room of S.H.A.E.F. which, as the Allied forces advanced, liaised with Delmer through Lt. Commander McLachlan and Squadron Leader Hodgkin.

Whilst daily production peaked at one million copies, after the landings a shortage of paper caused the production to lessen in favour of 'Surrender leaflets', which by now had acquired a high barter value in the German lines! With the German surrender on May 7th 1945, No. 381 then became the last issue of the paper, a total of 159,898,973 copies having been produced. For this achievement, at a celebratory party in the print shop at Marylands, John Gibbs of the Luton News burst into the festivities wearing a suit entirely overprinted with 'Nachrichten' front pages!

Throughout the 'Nachrichten' period, dissemination of the newspaper was exclusively by the Munroe bomb, a laminated wax paper cylinder, 5 feet in length and 18 inches in diameter. Explosive strips along each side were attached to a fuse that then blew the container apart at a predetermined height. Typically, 80,000 leaflets could

Loading & distributing the leaflet bombs
Luton News

thereby be scattered over a square mile and the need for such a device had been realised early in the leaflet campaign, since the initial methods had left much to be desired. Often aircrew were required to hand feed bundles of leaflets through the flare chute of the aircraft and, if the tail gunner was detailed for the task, he had to leave his post and so render the aircraft dangerously vulnerable in hostile skies. The accuracy of such drops could also be disappointing, such that, if released at an incorrect height or during adverse weather conditions, those productions intended for France might flutter down in North Africa!

The French had first suggested the idea of a leaflet 'bomb', but neither the Air Ministry nor Department Electra House showed any interest and the proposal was duly forgotten. Later, Squadron Leader Morrison of the R.A.F. suggested a similar concept, but again he met with official indifference, except from the Americans. They realised the potential and through the efforts of Captain James Munroe perfected an improved version. This then became the principal means of disseminating propaganda via the special leaflet squadron, flying B17s. Finally the British realised how effective the bomb could be and, in October 1944, a supply was duly ordered from America.

Seen on the previous page loading the leaflet bombs, after the war Andy Wilsher progressed to a senior position with the Luton News, published during his employment with the paper by Home Counties Newspapers Ltd. In this photograph he is seen at the age of 83.

CHAPTER NINE

SPECIAL COMMUNICATION UNITS

At the outbreak of war, enlisted into the Royal Signals several hundred radio amateurs were recruited for full time service at various stations both in Britain and abroad. They were then included amongst the personnel of Special Communication Units. Locally, SCU1 at Whaddon Hall dealt with 'subversive activities', controlling agents and training personnel for the handling of information from Bletchley Park. SCU 7 was based at Little Horwood, complete with the motor transport section, workshops and an operators training school. Operating from Hanslope Park, SCU3 monitored German wireless traffic.

SCU1 AND SCU7, WHADDON AND LITTLE HORWOOD

As the head of MI6, just before the war Admiral Sir Hugh Sinclair, 'C', decided to enlarge the small S.I.S. radio communications section at Broadway, London and provide a network independent of the Foreign Office. He appointed Richard Gambier Parry, from Philco Radio, to organise the department. When Sinclair died, at the end of 1939, he was succeeded by Colonel Stuart Menzies, who retained this position for many years.

With the increased risk of bombing, in 1939 the organisation moved from Broadway to Whaddon Hall, in Buckinghamshire, although even here was not entirely safe from enemy action, for amongst other incidents a bomb fell on the outskirts, near Shenley Church End, and another by the Beachampton Road.

For reasons of security, documents were taken daily from Bletchley Park and Whaddon to Whitehall by motorcycle despatch rider, and George Reeday was one of those engaged on this duty. For the role, he wore a blue armband and a white armband. If the blue armband was uppermost, he couldn't be stopped by the police and was fully authorised to shoot in self defence.

Initially known as Special Signals Unit No. 1, with the administration section housed in hutted accommodation, in 1939 Whaddon Hall, now as Special Communication Unit 1, became the headquarters of all the Special Communication Units and operated a transmitting and receiving station, known as 'Whaddon Main Line' in the grounds. Colonel Gambier Parry maintained and often used a room at the Hall, although for much of the war he actually lived at Wavendon Towers.

The role of the Unit was primarily to transmit information decoded by Bletchley Park to military commanders overseas and, built on concrete bases, two huts with low brick walls and a curved corrugated iron roof were constructed at the beginning of the war on a hilltop, near to Whaddon church. For self evident reasons the location soon became known as Windy Ridge and was in fact the Special Operations Group of SCU1, comprising a radio operating hut and a teleprinter hut, linked by landline to Hut 3 at Bletchley Park. In the surrounding field was erected a consequent array of

Whaddon Hall

The administration section were accommodated in huts behind the Hall and the three huts shown in the top right of the wartime photograph were respectively a teleprinter hut, radio hut – linked to the transmitting station at Tattenhoe Bare – and a rest room, the operators working shifts.

Richard Gambier Parry

Born in 1894 at Cirencester, Gloucestershire, Richard Gambier Parry was the second son of Grace and Sidney Gambier Parry, an architect. Educated at Eton, during World War One Richard served with distinction in the Royal Welch Fusiliers, being wounded three times and mentioned in despatches twice. He later joined the Royal Flying Corps and after the war between 1926 and 1931 found employment in the Public Relations Department of the B.B.C. Whilst working for the Philco Company, just before World War Two he was recruited by the Secret Intelligence Service to organise their radio communications. Twice divorced, in 1944 he married his secretary, Lisa Towse, daughter of Colonel H. Towse of the Royal Scots Guards. After the war Richard was appointed Director of Communications at Hanslope Park and he retired at the end of 1955, being knighted the following year. He then played an active role in local affairs as well as running a successful casino in Malta. After a long illness he died at his home in Abbots Close, in the village of Milton Keynes, on June 19th, 1965 and a well-attended memorial service took place in the village church. Floral decorations by Mrs. D. Smith recalled his First World War associations with the Royal Welch Fusiliers and the R.F.C., and in the address Canon Curtis aptly likened him to Falstaff, 'ever a quick and witty companion, with a gusto for life and living'. (Mrs. R. Healey)

receiving aerials, mainly dipoles and Marconi end fed wires. Possibly poles for the aerials came from Whaddon Chase which, some centuries before, during another conflict had supplied some 2000 poles for another use, namely fortifying Newport Pagnell as a Parliamentary garrison during the Civil War.

Adjoining the huts, a large generator was installed to provide emergency power. In normal operation electrical power came from the village supply, provided by the Northampton Electric Light Company, carried by lead-covered, unsheathed cable to a transformer in a field behind the village pub.

Information from Bletchley Park was received in the teleprinter hut and then encoded on handwritten paper sheets. These were passed to the radio operators' hut which contained twenty operating positions, or 'bays', each equipped with a National H.R.O. receiver, a morse key and headphones. At one end of the hut lay an extensive antenna distribution panel and in front of this sat the supervisor. He could thereby select and connect the transmitting and receiving aerials to a particular operator. The actual transmitting station for Windy Ridge was situated at Tattenhoe Bare, where tragically one of the operators was accidently electrocuted. In circumstances rather more mysterious, after the war, in April 1963 a large striped balloon carrying an R.A.F. officer in an open gondola landed in a field adjoining the old radio station, but, despite

Windy Ridge

In the early stage of the war, in the field below Whaddon church two huts were built. One received information via landline from Hut 3, at Bletchley Park. The other sent this coded information to overseas military commanders, via the nearby radio transmitting station at Tattenhoe Bare. Only the concrete base of the huts now remains. The exposed and elevated situation of the huts accounted for the name, Windy Ridge! For a while, in the nearby vicarage was housed the accounts department of S.C.U.1, Whaddon Hall. (J. Taylor)

Tattenhoe Bare

In order to minimise interference with the receiving aerials at Windy Ridge, the transmission station was situated a mile or so away at Tattenhoe Bare. Here staff also monitored the signals being keyed in at Windy Ridge, to ensure that the operators complied with the correct operating procedures. (J. Taylor)

enquiries being made, all the local R.A.F. stations denied any knowledge of the incident!

The radio operators had to be able to send Morse code at a rate of at least 22 words a minute, and two shift systems were worked, 0800 – 1600 and 1600 – 2200. Staff based at Tattenhoe Bare monitored the messages to ensure that the operators complied with the correct operating procedures. Mostly the 100 or so personnel were supplied by the army, but also included were 12 members from the air force and one from the navy, resplendent in bell bottoms!

Accommodation was initially provided in the Jubilee Hall of the village where, since their evacuation on September 2nd 1939, girls from the North Paddington Central School had been educated. As the numbers of army personnel increased, Nissen huts (the concrete bases of which still remain) were erected in the field behind the Hall, which now became the cookhouse. For local recreation the soldiers had the benefit of the village pub, the Lowndes Arms, and perhaps it was opportune that new lavatories had been installed during February 1939.

Apart from the Bletchley Park traffic, Whaddon also served as the radio communications centre for British embassies, and from stations at Calverton

In the surrounding fields reminders of the wartime use may still be found, in this case an aerial insulator. (J. Taylor)

116

Jubilee Hall, Whaddon

Initially the hall was used as a school for girls evacuated from London. Soon the army requisitioned the building as firstly a billet for soldiers and then, as the number of personnel increased, as a cookhouse, the soldiers being transferred to huts constructed in the field behind the hall. (J. Taylor. Vehicles by courtesy of Bletchley Park)

Weald and Nash maintained communication with agents abroad. The personnel included a mix of S.I.S. and army, mostly Royal Corps of Signals, including a local apprentice blacksmith from the Bletchley firm of Rowlands, who had initially been sent out to India but on arrival, being made a batman to an officer, he then found himself directed to Whaddon!

Equipped with workshops, the outbuildings of Whaddon Hall became a centre for the manufacture of radio sets for secret agents, and, located around a courtyard, the stables were used to store the items needed for the manufacture of the radio apparatus. These included imported equipment, components, generators, batteries and even the briefcases and rucksacks in which the agents equipment would be hidden whilst on active service. Completed items from the production unit were also stored.

Ewart Holden

The stores were the responsibility of Ewart Holden, who before the war had owned a radio shop in Twickenham. His friend Alex 'Polly' Pollard, a radio company salesman, who regularly called at the shop, had initially recommended him and, as Ewart's deputy, Horace Pidgeon became responsible for the actual storage and issue of the equipment. Most of the stores personnel came from the Royal Corps of Signals but, while training to be a wiring engineer, in 1941 Ken Bromley found his artistic talents recognised as being suitable for a

117

Calverton Weald

Above: Stationed for several weeks during 1945 at Calverton Weald, Clifford Taylor shows his grandaughter, Rebekah, around the remains of the station. Associated with Whaddon Hall, the radio station at Calverton Weald, complete with emergency diesel generator, office accommodation and sleeping quarters, maintained contact with agents in Occupied Europe. Below: Rebekah indicates the location of the long, rectangular hut, within which radio operators transmitted messages to agents overseas, and constantly listened for incoming signals. The foundation of the walls may still be traced, and in the field to the left would have been an extensive array of aerials. (J. Taylor)

Whaddon from the air

In the upper photo, Whaddon church may be seen in the centre. Immediately below in Church Field, on Windy Ridge lie the concrete bases of two huts. One received information from Bletchley Park, via a direct line, and the other sent this intelligence to the radio transmitting station at Tattenhoe Bare. Whaddon Hall, headquarters of Special Communications Unit 1, is seen upper top left. In the lower photo, Whaddon Hall is top right and in the centre lies Jubilee Hall, behind which may be seen the concrete bases of the accommodation huts for the personnel. In the lower left of the photo stands Whaddon church. (Mr. T. Trainor, Mr. P. Whitehead)

draughtsman. Indeed, as a fine cartoonist and artist, one of his paintings graced the bar of the Cock Hotel at Stony Stratford.

Tommy Fisher. Originally trained to be a wiring engineer, Ken Bromley's talents as an artist were soon recognised. This lino cut is a caricature of one of his colleagues, Tommy Fisher! (W. Dunkley)

At Whaddon, important research departments devised many new and novel items of equipment and these included the S phone, a line of sight radio transmitter and receiver that enabled agents on the ground to communicate with rendezvous aircraft, without the signals being detected. Fitted with the first set, based at the nearby Cranfield aerodrome, Fairey Battle, L4975, successfully completed the initial tests in May 1941.

In view of the secrecy and importance of the work being carried out at Whaddon, a Signals Security unit operated from the top floor of the Hall, where graffitti remains to be seen, carved into the woodwork!

The training wing for SCU1 was at Manor Farm, Little Horwood, with SCU7, at the same location, taking operators for advanced instruction. Nissen huts provided accommodation, and the centre was universally known as 'Gees', after the London building contractor who built the premises as a hunting lodge and stables in the 1930s. He was in fact Mr. George Gee, of the building firm Gee, Walker and Slater Ltd., who died, aged 50, in February 1943. Only a few days before, he had donated £250 to the Wolverton Merchant Navy Week, as a thanks offering for the safe return of

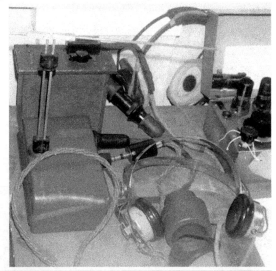

The 'S' Phone

Amongst the many secret projects at Whaddon, the 'S' Phone provided line of sight communication between rendezvous aircraft and secret agents and reception committees on the ground.
(Mr. R. W. Clarke (- sketch), Mr. D. White - photograph)

Entrance to Whaddon Hall

An arch once spanned the breadth between the two gate lodges. This had to be demolished at the beginning of the war to allow the passage of army vehicles. (J. Taylor. Vehicle by courtesy of Bletchley Park)

himself and his wife from a visit to America, and many Italian P.O.W.s, who had been set to work on the surrounding land, attended his funeral. In fact, despite the secrecy of the work at Manor Farm, it was not unknown for Italian P.O.W.s to wander in from the fields and peer through the windows!

At Little Horwood the S.C.U. personnel were mainly operators but with the occasional intake of drivers and cooks. Under the command of Captain Castleman, his secretary being Aubrey Green, the large workshop located at the rear of Manor Farm was staffed by Royal Signals instrument mechanics, bussed in daily from billets in Stony Stratford. As at Whaddon, the workshops manufactured secret communications equipment, including the Mark 5 and the later Mark 7 agents radio sets. Also produced would be the Mark 3 transmitter of 'astonishing range' which came to be standard equipment for the Special Liaison Units, attached to military commands overseas, specifically to handle the radio traffic associated with Bletchley Park.

At Little Horwood, Ted Turner and his team had the twin tasks of calibration and testing of all the manufactured items. Unsuited for frontline duties, some of the personnel were men aged over fifty and they included a mix of teachers, office workers, G.P.O. and businessmen. Despite the military overtones, military life was relaxed. The only parades were those of the 'pay parade' from WO11 Bert Norman, when the queue for pay took place outside the C.O.s office, received with the usual military salute.

Including those of research and development, he held overall charge of the workshops at Whaddon and Little Horwood, and under him Charlie West oversaw the

121

SCU1 personnel at Little Horwood

SCU1 personnel outside the workshops at Manor Farm, Little Horwood, in 1943. A goat, the mascot, may be seen centre, front row! (W. Dunkley)

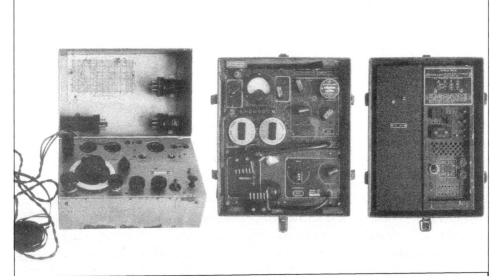

Clandestine radio equipment, for use by agents operating in Occupied Europe, was designed and built at the workshops in Little Horwood and Whaddon. Illustrated are the 'Paraset' - left, and the Type 3 Mk. II suitcase set, - right. (Mr. J. Elgar-Whinney)

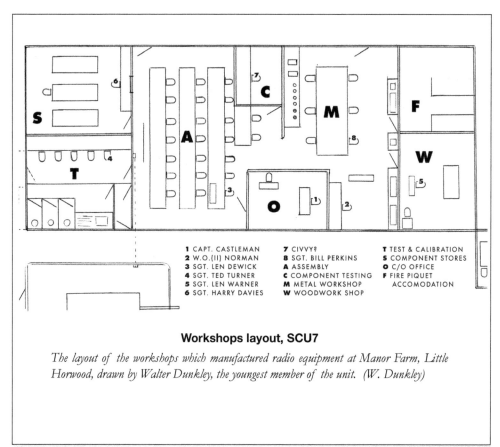

Workshops layout, SCU7

The layout of the workshops which manufactured radio equipment at Manor Farm, Little Horwood, drawn by Walter Dunkley, the youngest member of the unit. (W. Dunkley)

Legend:

1 CAPT. CASTLEMAN
2 W.O.(II) NORMAN
3 SGT. LEN DEWICK
4 SGT. TED TURNER
5 SGT. LEN WARNER
6 SGT. HARRY DAVIES
7 CIVVY?
8 SGT. BILL PERKINS
A ASSEMBLY
C COMPONENT TESTING
M METAL WORKSHOP
W WOODWORK SHOP
T TEST & CALIBRATION
S COMPONENT STORES
O C/O OFFICE
F FIRE PIQUET ACCOMODATION

The SCU personnel came from all walks of life, from schoolteachers to chemists. Walter Dunkley was the youngest member, seen on the left, and beside him is Alan Smith. (W. Dunkley)

Military vehicles outside the former workshops at Manor Farm, Little Horwood

The boiler house, complete with tall chimney, is seen in the background, tended during the war by 'Patsy' Duggan. Allegedly somewhat of a law unto himself, he also managed to be involved in a lorry crash at Little Horwood in October 1941. (J. Taylor. Vehicles courtesy of Bletchley Park)

The former SCU stores at Manor Farm, Little Horwood

From here, personnel would be issued with their uniforms and 'kit'. At the entrance to the road, until recently the 'jail hut' still remained, complete with bars at the windows! (J. Taylor. Vehicles courtesy of Bletchley Park)

Associated during the war with Special Communication activities, Manor Farm, Little Horwood, has been subject to much recent redevelopment. Now demolished, this building was the guardhouse. (J. Taylor)

chassis and metalwork aspects. Visits would often be made by Brigadier Gambier Parry, usually once a month, who sometimes arrived in his white painted Whitley aircraft. This came into land at the nearby Little Horwood airfield, although presumably not on the day that a flight of badly shot up American B17s made an emergency landing there.

The routine electrical maintenance of the Unit, including the outstations, was carried out by the Ewings, father and son, who lived in the village of Nash, whilst transport arrangements, both for vehicle maintenance and personnel movements, were dealt with by the M/T section based at Little Horwood. A small fleet of American Packard vehicles provided transport for the individual use of high ranking officials, and, with radio equipment installed in the rear passenger section, they were also used for the training of personnel on mobile exercises.

Solely in connection with the European operations, as the war progressed SCU8 with SLU8 were established at Little Horwood during March/April 1944, and at Whaddon the Special Liaison Unit radio vans were fitted out in the preparations for D Day. Staffed by British military operators, a Special Liaison Unit would be attached to each army headquarters and, as a mobile radio unit receiving the decodes from Bletchley Park, each was equipped with a large army van, fitted with two way W/T radios. At the time of D Day the whole of the personnel were put on full alert and in a departure from normal proceedings were obliged to wear full uniform and carry firearms. Even Windy Ridge was surrounded by armed personnel, in contrast to the usual tranquility.

With the war finally at an end, the duties of the Whaddon and Little Horwood units were transferred to Hanslope Park, to become the embryo Diplomatic Wireless Service, whilst Whaddon, for a while, found a new role as a collecting centre for documents retrieved from Germany. In one of the huts in the grounds mail bags were stacked high with such material, and in a bizarre irony, in view of the previous security, one of the personnel detailed to the archiving team was Anthony Blunt!

S.C.U.3, THE RADIO SECURITY SERVICE, HANSLOPE PARK

A t the beginning of the war there were obvious fears that enemy agents might be operating undercover in Britain, either transmitting reports on military manouevres or providing intelligence for bombing raids by the Luftwaffe. Locally, such concerns were indeed well founded, for, on the late afternoon of September 4th 1940, German agent number 3719 parachuted into the countryside near the Northamptonshire village of Denton. However, his descent was witnessed by a farm worker and, during imprisonment in Aylesbury jail, the agent duly revealed that his mission had been to transmit radio reports regarding activities in the area bordered by Oxford, Northampton and Birmingham. He was then given a simple ultimatum, either work for the British or be executed. He chose the former and provided further details concerning a second agent who, when parachuted into the same area four days later, was duly arrested and taken to Bozeat police station. He then transmitted for the British throughout the remainder of the war.

Indeed, through cunning and vigilance the British would control almost the entire

German spyring operating in Britain. Of course, the extent of German spy operations was unknown at the outbreak of the war, and under Major J. Worlledge, a signals officer in World War One, a small radio-monitoring department had been established to listen for enemy wireless transmissions. Yet not until Ralph Sheldon became involved did the organisation begin to achieve truly effective results. The managing director and owner of Hatch Manson wine merchants, in 1933 Sheldon had inherited the title of Lord Sandhurst and, being an enthusiastic radio amateur, his expertise now proved invaluable for his task of developing the Radio Security Service, as the monitoring organisation became known.

Linked by a direct teleprinter line to Bletchley Park, for their headquarters the R.S.S. took over vacant cells in C Block of Wormwood Scrubs prison and here, for ideas and suggestions, Sheldon conducted an important meeting with the aptly named Arthur Watts, President of the Radio Society of Great Britain. Of the opinion that the members of the Society would be ideally qualified to undertake a systematic monitoring, Watts arranged for them to become 'Voluntary Interceptors' in an organisation under the War Office initially known as 'The Illicit Wireless Intercept Organisation'.

At the outbreak of the war, the transmitters of radio amateurs had been impounded but not shortwave receivers. Receiving radio sets were also issued on loan from the War Office but only on the understanding that 'Local radio dealers should not be called in to effect repairs'.

In addition to the three small intercept stations set up by the Post Office at Land's End, John O'Groats and on the cliffs of Dover, 'V.I.s' would become an essential part of the R.S.S. and eventually replaced the intercept posts. If a V.I. achieved a minimum performance each month, then exemption would apply from having to perform otherwise enforceable duties. As described to the 'V.I.s', the object of their organisation was 'to intercept, locate and close down illicit wireless stations operated either by enemy agents in Great Britain or by persons not necessarily enemy agents operating transmitting stations without being licensed to do so under the Defence Regulations, 1939.' As for their role, eventually to number 1500 plus, 'Voluntary interceptors were spaced throughout the country in the main centres of population and elsewhere, working either singly or in groups, for as many hours a day as their civilian vocations allow them. They are asked to furnish intercept logs, daily wherever possible but, in any case, three times weekly. Information less frequently furnished will, in war time, be of little value.'

In the event of illicit stations being detected, they would then be geographically located with the help of the Post Office, which had a fleet of direction finding vans. Apart from monitoring wireless traffic, interceptors were also asked to listen for suspicious gossip in their neighbourhood and to look out for unusual aerials in the vicinity. Intercepted transmissions were initially sent to Wormwood Scrubs but, with the prison bombed and the risk of increased air raids, premises were instead secured in the village of Arkley, near Barnet, this also being more suited to cope with the increasing amount of intercepts.

By March 1940, it had become apparent that no enemy signals were being transmitted from Britain and instead attention turned to those being received from the Continent. Controlled by Regional Officers, who further divided their region between Group Leaders, the Voluntary Interceptors were therefore retained and soon began to achieve an increasing success. Indeed, within the first three months, not only had 600 agents been discovered on the Continent but members of the R.S.S. had also unofficially decoded transmissions by the German Secret Service, the Abwehr. This feat naturally attracted the attention, if not benevolent, of the head of the S.I.S. (Secret Intelligence Service) communications section – MI8 'Section VIII' – Felix Cowgill, newly appointed from the Indian Police in Calcutta, and he now began moves to bring the R.S.S. under S.I.S. control.

Before the war S.I.S. lacked an extensive and efficient radio network and in remedy Admiral Sinclair, 'C', head of the S.I.S., decided to set up his own, free of interference by the Foreign Office. From a previous employment at the Philco radio company, he chose Colonel Richard Gambier Parry to run the organisation, and in May 1941 the R.S.S. was removed from the War Office, with MI8 transferred from MI5 to MI6, the R.S.S. now being MI8 (C) of MI8. With the overseas section designated Special Communications Unit 4, the R.S.S. now became known as Special Communications Unit 3 and, with several subsidiaries, including outposts at Forfar, Arkley, St. Erth and Leatherhead, 'liberally financed and equipped', the operation centred on Hanslope Park. A country mansion in North Buckinghamshire, this had been purchased, for secret radio communication purposes, by the Foreign Office at the same time as Bletchley Park, and from June 1941 the organisation duly reported to Gambier Parry. As his deputy, he appointed a fellow Etonian and personal friend, Colonel Edward Maltby, to take charge, and accordingly the staff began to arrive.

During August 1941, the administration workers took up their duties and in the following month the first of the radio operators, Wilfred Limb and William Chittleburgh, began their tasks, the first being to clean out the corn bins. These then provided a primary accommodation for six H.R.O. radio communication receivers, arranged on trestle tables. Perhaps this was not ideal but results were soon achieved. From the volumes of traffic being intercepted at Bletchley Park, G.C. & C. S. were able, in December 1941, to break the Enigma cipher of the Abwehr, and without this knowledge the success of the 'Double Cross' system, controlling the German spies in Britain, would not have been possible. In fact during 1941, the R.S.S. was directly responsible for the capture of five of the 23 agents sent to the U.K. and the identification of two others.

The corn bins at Hanslope continued in use until the nearby intercept station at 'The Lodge', Bullington End, staffed by 115 radio amateurs, became fully operational in 1942. Bletchley Park then took over the running and, from Whaddon Hall, the newly promoted Brigadier Gambier Parry now controlled the clandestine radio communications with countries to include France, Belgium, Holland and Norway. Directed by Major Dick Keen, within the U.K. nine radio direction finding systems, including Hanslope, were an integral feature of the R.S.S. operation, and to the various direction finding stations the operators could transmit instructions via a morse key connected to a common landline. As for the radio receivers, they were fed by an extensive system of aerials, and the centre maintained a round the clock vigilance.

Ultimately destined for Bletchley Park, encoded in S.I.S. ciphers, intelligence was sent to Hanslope from Colonel Bertrand's ultra secret base in a remote French chateau. Gleaned mainly from line taps on the main telephone routes to Berlin, between March 1st 1941 and November 5th 1942 some 2748 messages would be transmitted, but inevitably the German radio location vans began to home in on the French centre.

Officially Hanslope opened in May 1942 and, although Captain Prickett was the first Commanding Officer, with his greater appreciation of the needs a radio amateur, Reginald Wigg, soon became his replacement.

By early 1943, Hanslope began to intercept unidentified stations transmitting from the immediate area, but the operators were by necessity in ignorance that these were in fact the 'black' propaganda broadcasts, being transmitted from the secret radio stations at Potsgrove and Gawcott. On enquiry to the B.B.C., Colonel Maltby was discreetly referred to the wireless technical director of the S.I.S., who thereon arranged to keep him informed of all future schedules.

Apart from the radio monitoring, at Hanslope Park other secret activities included the manufacture of the 'Rockex' system, for enciphering top grade British telegraph signals. A need also became apparent to provide a means for speech encipherment since, via a large antenna near Eindhoven, the Germans routinely monitored telephone calls transmitted across the Atlantic. Greatly involved in this project was Alan Turing, who had been invaluable in the codebreaking activities at Bletchley Park. From his lodgings with Mrs. Ramshaw, in the village of Shenley Brook End, for two days a week during the course of six months he cycled over to Hanslope to work on the project, assisted by the several staff assigned to him. In late summer 1944, he then gave up his Shenley lodgings and moved to a room on the top floor of the Hanslope mansion, before transferring to a cottage in the walled kitchen garden. As for the speech encipherment project, known as 'Delilah', although complete by the spring of 1945 the Post Office now had a device of their own and this gained preference, despite the many merits of 'Delilah', which was dismissed as 'too crackly'.

The competence of Hanslope gained such renown that, accompanied by Brigadier Gambier Parry, many persons of contemporary eminence, to include Lord Gort, General Alexander, Field Marshall Montgomery and General Eisenhower, were all variously shown around the centre.

By September 1944, although the end of the war was in sight, for the V.I.s the dangers of complacency were well appreciated. In order to guard against this, an official circulation emphasised the need for their continued vigilance for 'It is appreciated that with the stand down of the Home Guard and the reduction of demands on other Civil Defence workers, there is a tendency for some V.I.s to ease up on their work, which is regretted. You must be aware that all Civil Defence workers are concerned with duties affecting this country only, whereas the work of V.I.s covers the whole of Europe and will continue so long as fighting lasts and possibly after that. Please carry on the good work and support our lads at the front.'

After the war, incorporating the Whaddon units, Hanslope Park then became the centre for handling all Foreign Office radio traffic and operated under the title the Diplomatic Wireless Service, remaining as a Government communications centre to this day.

Hanslope Park, SCU3

After the war Hanslope Park became a centre for the Diplomatic Wireless Service, handling Foreign Office radio communications with British Embassies abroad. (Mr. P. Benge)

CHAPTER TEN

AN AERIAL VIEW

The region accommodated, throughout the war, several factories and establishments engaged either in the manufacture of aircraft components or the repair and assembly of aeroplanes. In addition, airfields were constructed, crews trained and secret work undertaken, from the testing of airborne communications equipment to the flight trials of prototype fighters.

Secretly, at least from the enemy, aircraft repairs and assembly were carried out during the war at Wolverton Works, to include such types as Whitley bombers. Wings for Horsa gliders were made, repairs were carried out to the wings of Hawker Typhoons, and, in other work to assist the war effort, gun sights, tank wheels and parts, bailey bridges and rifle butts, and over 8,000 collapsible assault landing craft were manufactured. Certainly Wolverton had good reason to assist the war effort, since when enemy bombs were dropped on the town, a baby was blown from its pram right across a street. Miraculously the infant survived unharmed.

As part of the wartime production, the manufacture of aero components, including magnetos and spark plugs, assumed a national importance and, with the Ministry of Labour having requisitioned a part of the Peake's clothing factory in Bletchley, the W.I.C.O.s Electrical Company and Pacey and Co. now occupied this accommodation. Primarily an American firm, W.I.C.O.s manufactured magnetos, and had originally

The wings for troop and equipment carrying Horsa gliders, as deployed in the Arnhem and D Day landings, were manufactured at Wolverton Works. This picture is displayed at the Milton Keynes Museum, which contains much information regarding the wartime role of the Works. (Milton Keynes Museum)

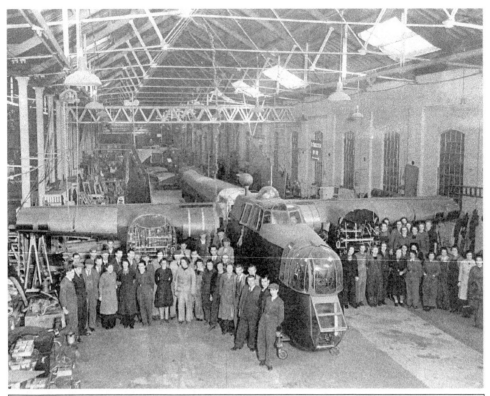

Facilities in the district were engaged in the repair and assembly of aircraft. Whitley bombers are seen here at the Wolverton railway works. (Milton Keynes Museum)

The Short Stirling was a bomber built to an R.A.F. specification that limited the wingspan to pass through the doors of the standard size hangers. This reduced the aircrafts operational altitude, causing a withdrawal from front line duties. Stirlings were then flown in and parked on the grounds of Woburn Abbey for storage and maintenance, being later used in the role of glider tugs. (Keith Coleman)

been established in London to look after the European market. With the outbreak of war, it then became a British company associated with Messrs. Pacey and Co., manufacturers of spark plugs, and demand became so great that, to house the machinery sent down from London, a new factory was built further along Denbigh Hall Road.

Yet activities of a more clandestine nature were taking place nearby. As mentioned in a previous chapter, the typesetting of the early propaganda leaflets was undertaken in the grounds of Woburn Abbey on equipment installed in the former hanger of the 'Flying Duchess', and continuing this association was later transferred to the 'model hospital' of her foundation, at Marylands. The 'Flying Duchess' was in fact Mary, wife of the 11th Duke of Bedford, who had shown an early aptitude for mechanical matters by taking an interest in motoring, dispensing with the services of a chauffeur and even undertaking the running repairs herself. In 1926 she took her first aeroplane flight and, suffering from tinnitus but finding that the experience relieved this affliction, then developed a keen interest in flying. For two years she flew as a passenger in a hired aircraft but then began flying instruction at the age of 62.

The 'Flying Duchess', Mary, the wife of the 11th Duke of Bedford, in her flying gear c.1930. She began flying lessons at the age of 62 and a hanger to accommodate her biplane aircraft was constructed in the grounds of Woburn Abbey. With the outbreak of war, this was then used to accommodate the typesetting equipment for the layout of the early propaganda leaflets. (His Grace the Duke of Bedford and the Trustees of the Bedford Estates)

At the age of 71, on the afternoon of March 22nd 1937, she took off from Woburn on a cross country flight but, after several hours, the alarm was raised when she did not return. After a few days, wreckage from her aircraft was washed up on the east coast, though it provided no clue as to the cause of the fateful crash. During the war, the grounds of Woburn Abbey became a storage park for obsolete Stirling bombers, flown in by pilots using the now demolished chimneys of the nearby brickworks at Ridgmont as an aid to unorthodox touchdown! With the bombers maintained in a serviceable condition, they were later used on glider towing duties.

Whilst the grounds of Woburn Abbey would be used as a makeshift 'airfield', the prospects of war led to a need for additional operational airfields and the localities became chosen for those at Cranfield and Wing. The testing of the 'S Phone', at Cranfield, has already been described, the aerodrome having opened on June 1st 1937, as part of No. 1 Group. With war declared, under No. 6 Group it then became a Group

Pool, providing replacement personnel and aircraft for the Advanced Air Striking Force in France, and, as the war progressed, the airfield became a target for several Luftwaffe raids. In August 1940, 52 bombs were dropped on the neighbourhood and on September 24th a parachute mine exploded in a field near the town, damaging several houses and shops in the High Street. Towards the close of the war, a V1 then fell some 800 yards from the officers' mess.

In the early stage of the war, Cranfield had been transferred to No. 23 Group, Flying Training Command, and a decision was then made that the unit should be only concerned with twin engined aircraft. In 1944 Mosquitos were duly introduced and since Guy Gibson, of 'Dambusters' fame, had been the station commander for a while, perhaps this was somewhat ironic, as it was in this type of aircraft that he was killed on active service during the same year. The loss of another famous personality then occurred when the plane carrying Glenn Miller to France disappeared without trace, having taken off from the satellite ground to Cranfield, at Twinwoods Farm. After the war, the Empire Test Pilots School arrived from Boscombe Down, and since the College of Aeronautics had been opened at Cranfield in October 1946, then transferred to Farnborough in August 1947.

There is an added local poignancy to the tragic loss of Glenn Miller, as the pilot of the plane taking him to France, Johnny Morgan, had a date planned that evening with a young W.A.A.F. Flying Control Clerk working in the control tower at the Twinwoods Farm airfield; her name was Thelma Acton. In recent years Thelma came to live in Milton Keynes and rememberrd that she spent many happy nights dancing to the Glenn Miller Army Air Force Band, who were based in Bedford for several months. In the previous summer the Band were travelling through Twinwoods on a transit flight and during their wait the W.A.A.F.s suggested they put on a show, since they never had any entertainment. "The place was packed and there we were jitterbugging in front of the little stage they had put up," Thelma recalls. The cause of the aircraft's crash remains a mystery, although by one account the plane had strayed into an area at sea used by the R.A.F. to dump bombs that had not been dropped over the target. (Photo courtesy Milton Keynes Citizen.)

As for the airfield at Wing, and the associated airfield at Little Horwood, airborne tests of communication equipment were carried out, and agents trained in the use of the relevant apparatus. Wing airfield also became a centre for flight trials of the secret Martin Baker MB3 single engined fighter, equipped with 6 cannon and built to specification F.18/39.

First flown on August 31st 1942, on September 12th the aircraft unfortunately hit a haystack when the Napier Sabre engine seized on a landing approach, and in the ensuing crash the pilot, Captain Baker, was tragically killed.

Construction of the airfield had begun at the beginning of the war, utilising much Irish labour and horse and carts, and during the work, according to local memory, every Sunday a white German Dornier reconnaisance aircraft would fly over so low that the markings could clearly be seen. The plane soon became known as 'Jerry Sunday', but one day two Hurricane fighters were waiting, and the Dornier is supposed to have been shot down near Great Brickhill.

The airfield had opened on November 17th 1941, and amongst the first aircraft to land was an Airspeed Oxford. Unfortunately, the guard posted on duty was supposedly killed when a gust of wind lifted the tail of the aircraft and abruptly brought the nose down on him. Using 'war weary' Wellington bombers, the airfield became a part of 26 Operational Training Unit, formed on January 15th 1942, initially under 7 Group, and was used for 'crewing up', where pilots, navigators, wireless operators, bomb aimers and gunners met for the first time. After a short ground school, the pilots, wireless operators and gunners went to Little Horwood, where the pilots were converted to the aircraft doing circuits and bumps, and the crews were then reunited at Wing, carrying out consequent cross country practice flights, both day and night.

Inevitably, several crashes tragically occurred and on August 7th 1943, during a night training mission from Wing, a Wellington came in low from the surrounding countryside but, striking a walnut tree, then crashed near the High Street in the town of Winslow. Ripped off in the collision, a wing plummeted onto the roof of the Bletchley Co-op butchers and, careering over some houses, the rest of the aircraft demolished the Chandos Arms and smashed into Rose Cottages. Many people were killed, and a plaque affixed to the British Legion building, that came to occupy the site, would be placed to their memory.

On another occasion a Wellington, coming in to land one foggy November morning, hit the imposing water tower at Mursley, and all the crew were killed. A plaque alongside the tower now stands in their memory, and recalls details of the tragedy, even more poignant since not only did relatives of the crew attend the ceremony, but also because the tail gunner of the aircraft had only recently returned to duty following a previous crash.

The spectacular arrival of American aircraft occurred on January 23rd 1943, when, returning from a raid on L'Orient, a flight of badly shot up B17s, of the 91st Bombardment Group, made a forced landing at Little Horwood. With many dead and

With a satellite at Little Horwood, Wing airfield opened on November 17th, 1941, for the training of bomber crews.

Agents were also trained in the use of airborne communications equipment, for operating with the Resistance in Occupied Europe, and in more recent years another resistance campaign was launched when the Government tried to impose London's third airport on the region. A determined local opposition successfully thwarted this proposal, and on the outskirts of the old wartime airfield a monument now commemorates this achievement. (J Taylor/A Ainger)

Mursley Water Tower

For the wartime aircrews operating from Wing aerodrome, the nearby water tower at Mursley (opposite) provided a prominent landmark. Ninety-eight feet high, the tower, completed shortly before the outbreak of war, at a cost of £23,995, was filled from the pumping station at Battlesden and provided a reservoir for a large area of North and Central Bucks. Built for strength, it survived with minimal structural damage when hit by a Wellington bomber, which crashed into it on April 11th, 1943, whilst carrying out dual circuits and landings in fog. All the crew were killed and in 1995 a plaque to their memory was dedicated and placed near to the tower, recalling the incident and the names of the crew. Before the war, on a cross country flight a Fairey Swordfish crash landed in an adjacent field, across which a long furrow was gouged by the practice torpedo. (J. Taylor)

injured aboard, the casualties were then urgently rushed to the Royal Bucks Hospital at Aylesbury. Returning from a raid on Nantes, another battle damaged B17 crashed in a wood on the outskirts of Wing airfield on September 23rd 1943. Wounded by a flak burst, the pilot managed to nurse the damaged aircraft back to England and, despite some serious injuries, all the crew survived the crash.

At the end of the European war many aircraft were despatched to collect the thousands of liberated P.O.W.s, and being designated a receiving airfield, some 819 men were brought to Wing in 33 Dakotas on April 9th 1945. Tragically, on May 10th a Lancaster carrying more P.O.W.s crashed on landing, but, more happily, the pilot of another Lancaster, having flown to Brussels to collect 24 prisoners, on arrival found amongst the thousands of men milling about an old friend from his training days in New Zealand!

On March 4th 1946, 26 O.T.U. closed and on May 4th Maintenance Command took control. With the aircraft withdrawn, the site was then used as a bomb dump, stacked with 'miles and miles' of all types of munitions. Their disposal took place over several years and of the personnel involved in this operation, Mr. Ian Pennington, now resident in Wales, describes his role:

Central Ammunition Field Storage) Buckingham

CAD (FS) Buckingham RAOC was originally formed at, or soon after, the end of WWII and comprised a Headquarters Camp at Tingewick providing accommodation and administration for the military personnel, both Royal Army Ordnance Corps and Royal Pioneer Corps, employed on the three ex wartime airfield locations at Hinton in the Hedges, Horwood and Finmere.

CAD (FS) BKM was used for the storage of obsolete and unwanted ammunition and explosives left over from WW II and was scheduled for closure. The ammunition was stored on the runways, perimeter taxi ways and aircraft parking lots in IG Shelters.

(Iron Galvanised Shelters – open ended small Nissen Huts).

Horwood sub-depot was involved in the disposal of Cartridges BL (canvas bags of propellent with gunpowder igniters), Carts 25pr, Mines Anti-Personnel, Guncotton and Carts 40mm.

Carts 25pr had the primers and propellent removed. The primers were disposed of in a prototype semi-continuous firing machine and the empty primers and cartridge cases declared free from explosive and sent for scrap brass. The Mines AP had the mines removed. The mines were then packed for deep sea dumping and the cast iron mortars sent for scrap. The Carts 40mm were of the old 40/60 type used in the wartime Bofors light AA gun. These were to be packed for deep sea dumping but, prior to final packing, had to be checked for mazak poisoning. The fuses on these rounds were made from a zinc alloy that prior to, and also subsequently to, anodising were liable to deterioration to powder form

….. mazak poisoning. Each round had to be checked for deterioration and the offending fuse removed for local disposal at Finmere. Some of these fuses could not be removed due to the powderous state. An old hand, a civilian former Ammunition Examiner, was asked for advice and showed the operator on the line that the simplest way to deal with the problem was to take hold of the complete round by the brass cartridge case and give the fuse end a sharp tap on the edge of the bench. This method worked successfully until one such fuse hit the deck and the detonator went off. No injuries, no damage, but a short sharp shock and a quick trip back to the drawing board. Subsequently, all rounds in a similar state went to Finmere.

Carts BL (Cartridges Breech Loading) were generally for larger calibre guns, 5.5in Field Gun, 6in Coastal Defence Gun and 7in (or was it 7.5in) Howitzer. These BL Carts comprised a stitched canvas bag of the appropriate diameter and of various lengths containing loose pellets or sticks of propellent with a red cloth gunpowder igniter stitched on one or both ends. The traditional method of disposal for Carts BL was to lay the carts on the surface to the explosive limit prescribed, then to be remotely ignited from a place of safety.

This method of disposal was not considered fast enough to complete the closure on schedule. Therefore the prototype Semi-Continuous Propellent Burner was designed and put to use at Horwood. The set up comprised an IG shelter with two side doors, one for each of the two internal compartments which had an internal bulkhead with a hatch between the two compartments. Each end was sealed by a wall, each having a built in hatch.

This shelter sat on the top of a steep bank on the northern side of the airfield. At the bottom of the bank a brick grate was built with some rather large boiler fire bars inset. Connecting this grate with the shelter at the top was a steel chute.

The procedure was that the rear compartment was filled through the external hatch one round at a time until the magazine, as it was called, was filled to the explosive limit.

The two operators, one in each compartment, would then act as follows:-

(i) The magazine operator would open the internal hatch and pass one cartridge through to the operator at the top of the chute. He, once the internal hatch was closed, would (ii) open the external hatch at the top of the chute and push the cartridge through and close the hatch. The cartridge would then slide down the chute into a grate wherein a fire had been lit with scrap wood. The igniter on the cartridge would then set the cartridge alight. This procedure being repeated whilst stocks were available.

I was in charge of this contraption for a while and modified the procedure by loading the magazine through the side door. Work proceeded at a much faster rate but that raised a few eyebrows. I got a severe telling off, the working instructions were amended and a certain senior rank took the credit! So what's new?

Guncotton was also disposed of at Horwood though not by demolition. The procedure here was to break down the 1lb slabs into small pieces, then to be mixed with waste oils and burnt in steel trays cut from 45 gal oil drums. This breakdown was carried in warm water because the amount of desensitiser present was an unknown quantity.

More than that, it was known that guncotton could burn to detonation, hence the breakdown into small pieces. Unfortunately, on one occasion one burn of GC had not broken down to small enough pieces and there was an explosion. Fortunately, it was not a large one and there were no casualties, only a rather surprised operator.

Ah! Happy Days!

Dramatically emphasizing the peril of the large amounts of ammunition that were stockpiled in the local region, after the war in July 1946, a motorcyclist crashed into an ammunition dump on the Woburn Road, near Millbrook. The dump immediately blew up, with shrapnel and debris raining down over a large area. Nine soldiers crept to within five yards of the dump and, sheltering behind a pile of gravel, turned a fire extinguisher onto the blaze. Two soldiers narrowly escaped injury when the rims of their steel helmets were blown off and the explosions, rattling windows for many miles, continued for over two hours.

APPENDIX A

BLETCHLEY PARK – 'THE BIG SISTER'

Bletchley Park was the 'big sister' of a family of secret intelligence organisations, removed to the local area mostly before the outbreak of World War Two as a refuge from the expected heavy bombing of London. The region had been chosen not only for the excellent road and rail links with the Capital but also the access, via the Fenny Stratford repeater station, to the national trunk cables network, which provided secure and instant communication between the local secret headquarters and the centres of Government and decision making. Very few people knew the overall structure or purpose of the clandestine organisations but nevertheless, to a certain extent they were all covertly interconnected and, as with most siblings, between Bletchley Park and her 'secret sisters' there were varying degrees of bonding.

Perhaps the strongest was that with the Radio Security Service, centred on Hanslope Park, which constantly monitored enemy radio transmissions and supplied this information for analysis by the codebreakers at Bletchley Park. When relevant, in a suitably disguised manner some of this information could then be passed to the propaganda organisation at Woburn Abbey, and one important occasion would be the revelation at a meeting, convened in the ballroom of Woburn Abbey, that the Germans were planning to invade Russia. This knowledge then allowed the propagandists sufficient time to prepare a suitable response, via their 'black' broadcasts transmitted to Occupied Europe from secret radio stations at Gawcott and Potsgrove. Reciprocally, when the codebreakers at Bletchley Park temporarily lost the ability to read the U boat signals, and the convoy losses became desperate, Bletchley Park urgently asked if the propaganda department could help, and in consequence the launch was brought forward of a radio station especially beamed at the U boats which, attracting the attention of the crews by musical entertainment, then weakened their morale through subtle disinformation inserted within the news breaks.

Ironically, Wrens, seconded for duties at Bletchley Park, were accommodated in several local country mansions including Woburn Abbey, but despite their close proximity remained completely oblivious to the existence of the propaganda department! Information gleaned by the propagandists, from refugees and other sources, might often be of value to the codebreakers by confirming, reinforcing or illuminating their deciphered intelligence, and similarly, agents of the Special Operations Executive, which locally operated a training centre at Chicheley Hall and communication centres at Poundon and Grendon Underwood, were ideally placed to provide further information. In turn, Bletchley Park could warn them of dangerous situations, or request that they concentrate on a contemporary matter of interest.

The information deciphered by Bletchley Park had to be made swiftly available to those military commanders best able to act upon it and this was the task of Special Communications Unit 1, based at Whaddon Hall. From nearby radio stations, highly competent personnel transmitted the intelligence to Special Liaison Units overseas, attached to the various military commands, and for obvious reasons of security only summaries of Ultra were transmitted, since a verbatim transcription could have compromised the entire secret. Trained at Bletchley Park, those heading each S.L.U. were sworn to absolute secrecy, and discreetly informed that if they should ever break the oath, they would be shot. At Little Horwood and Whaddon the design of secret and advanced radio apparatus was undertaken and, to maintain contact with Bletchley Park, in the preparations for D Day vehicles to accompany the advancing armies were especially fitted out with the necessary communications equipment. Such were the relations between Bletchley Park and the family of 'secret sisters', and, although many volumes have been written about the wartime achievement of the codebreakers, no book on local secret intelligence activities would be complete without briefly recalling the background of the major milestones, and some of the social aspects, as to how the personnel, many of whom were billeted in the town, integrated with the local community.

By the use of the Enigma cypher machine, developed initially for commercial use at the end of World War One, the Germans believed that they had a secure means of encoding their wireless communications. Thereby the importance they placed on the system proved an incentive for the French to glean details of the military adaptations, and towards this ambition they made contact with an agent, codenamed 'Asche', in the German Army, who was employed as a civil servant in the German Defence Ministry Cipher Office. On November 8th 1931, at Verviers, in Belgium, he met with a senior officer in French Intelligence and not only supplied the Instruction Manual for Enigma Operators, but also the Operators Enciphering Procedures. Yet, even so, the French decided that the system was unbreakable and when the information was shown to the British they considered the source too expensive and the danger of a war remote, 'the threat from Germany being neither certain nor immediate'. Disheartened, in the following month the French officer then made the documents known to the Poles whose response, since from 1923 they had been working on the problem with insubstantial success, proved more encouraging. In fact by 1933, through additional information supplied by 'Asche', they had entirely reconstituted the Enigma military version, and production of the machine began in Warsaw. From 1937 by their development of a cryptographic 'bombe' the rapid decoding of thousands of possible combinations greatly accelerated the process of decoding and, when the outbreak of war became inevitable, at a secret hideout in the underground concrete bunkers of Pyry Forest, near Warsaw, on July 25th 1939 at a meeting with 38 French and British experts they explained their methods of breaking the Enigma code. The Poles agreed to present an Enigma, plus technical drawings of the 'bombe', to the British and these were duly smuggled into Britain by diplomatic bag, brought from the British Embassy in Paris by a courier who at Victoria station was met by no less than the head of the Secret Intelligence Service, Colonel Menzies. With the invasion of Poland the Polish experts then joined with the French at a secret location, known as 'Bruno', 35 kilometres south east of Paris, and in December a returning British emissary bore the encouraging news that, on occasion, the army code had been broken. Until the Fall of France the British code breakers consequently worked closely with 'Bruno' and, following the French capitulation, continued their endeavours with singular success at Bletchley Park. Fortunately, the first British built 'bombe', used in the code-breaking process, and designed earlier in the year, became ready for use by the end of May 1940 and, with the work undertaken by the British Tabulating Machinery factory at Letchworth, the redesigned models proved even more powerful than the Polish type.

Destined to become the wartime headquarters of the codebreakers, the country estate of Bletchley Park had been purchased in 1883 by Herbert Leon, later created Sir Herbert Leon, a London financier, and after his death in 1926 his widow, Lady Fanny Leon, remained at the mansion until she died in 1937. Early in 1938 the interest was then purchased by a local syndicate led by a local builder, Hubert Faulkner, who proposed to demolish the mansion and redevelop the area as housing. However, with the imminence of war, the Secret Service had begun investigating locations to accommodate the Government Code and Cipher School as a refuge from the expected perils that awaited London, and in consequence Bletchley Park was instead privately purchased by Admiral Sir Hugh Sinclair, 'C' of the Secret Service, with the cost underwritten by the Chamberlain Government. A short while before the Munich Crisis, of September 1938, a series of trial runs to Bletchley Park from the codebreakers' headquarters at Broadway was then made, with the true nature of these journeys masked by the personnel masquerading as 'Captain Ridley's Hunting Party'. He was the man in charge of the move and, since it was anticipated that vast numbers of personnel would have to be employed, representing the Government, on November 25th 1938 he also paid an afternoon visit to the Mr. E.C. Cook, the headmaster of the Bletchley Road Senior School, and asked that an appointment should be made for the following Tuesday, when a deputation would arrive at the premises 'in order to ascertain its full accommodation, as in case of war it could probably be required for other purposes'. Mr. Cook duly referred the Captain to the Secretary for Education who on November 28th sent a letter instructing that the visit should be cancelled and the whole affair referred to the Secretary. On the following day Captain Ridley and a senior official again visited the school in the afternoon but on being handed the letter they departed and no more was heard about the matter.

As for Bletchley Park, codenamed 'Station X', in August 1939 a move proper from Broadway then took place and, branching off at Heath and Reach for the final leg to their new accommodation, the staff travelled down in 3 motor coaches. Hundreds of other personnel would also soon become acquainted with Bletchley but, as for their billeting arrangements in the town, for some of the early arrivals, as one landlady discovered, a swift correction of attitude seemed necessary since; 'My first people assumed I had become their handmaid and expected a full service, including breakfast in bed! I soon cured that, and the next lot could not have been nicer.' In fact householders were paid 21s for each person billetted with them and their obligatory guests therefore became known as the 'guinea pigs'! With all the available accommodation eventually taken at Bletchley, throughout the war billets were necessarily also found in many of the surrounding villages and towns including Bedford, to and from which personnel travelled in a special 3 coach train, nicknamed 'the Whitehall'.

From radio interceptions made at numerous and diverse locations, from the North of Scotland to Dorset, the first decodes of operational value became available during the Norwegian Campaign in April 1940, and as the information from Bletchley Park became more copious, urgent intercepts were sent by teleprinter to London, with the rest rushed through by despatch rider. The term 'Ultra', as applied to the Bletchley information, had been the name applied to the Admiral's code at Trafalgar, but for the Prime Minister the intelligence was known as 'Boniface', since the early decrypts were circulated in Whitehall as reports having been obtained from an agent of that name. However, the choosing of the name had not been arbitrary, for on June 6th the head of the Secret Intelligence Service had held a meeting to discuss the distribution and cover for the Ultra intelligence, and the day just happened to be the morrow of the feast day of St. Boniface, a martyred English missionary monk. Since his title within the church was the 'Apostle of Germany', this seemed the ideal intelligence cover!

In early 1940 the different Enigma systems, referred to by colours, were divided amongst the chief cryptanalysts, who were allocated huts in the grounds of the Bletchley mansion, although the initial construction of the temporary buildings had caused the local authority a problem, when found to contravene the Building Line. The Council then lodged a formal complaint and requested that in future such additions should comply with the regulations! Additional concerns had also been raised in October 1939 when the Bletchley Council Surveyor submitted an application to supply water for the temporary buildings. This then further aggravated an existing problem that the increasing demand on the town's water resource was starting to stir up iron deposits in the mains, leading to a discolouration of the supply. Nevertheless, the huts remained and a number were also constructed to accommodate those sections dealing with translation and interpretation.

As one of its initial achievements, Ultra would provide details of the speed of the German advance, and so allow time for the organisation of the 'little armada' for the evacuation of Dunkirk. The first tentative breaks had now also been made into the air force Enigma, and the War Office undertook the interception of these transmissions, mistakenly believing them to be army traffic. This would not become regularly available until April 1942, although from interceptions of the air force Enigma some indication of army movements could be made. At this critical time Ultra began to confirm the German policy of sending large fighter formations over Britain, so intending to entice up the R.A.F. and destroy more of their depleted numbers, and in fact on 'Eagle Day' via Hut 6 the decodes revealed the actual airfields threatened. Thus armed with this Bletchley information Air Chief Marshall Dowding, C. in C. of Fighter Command, merely met each challenge with a token squadron or two and, confined to his lonely knowledge of the Ultra secret, since he could not reveal the reason for his tactics for many years he would be denied due credit for his achievements in the Battle of Britain. With the R.A.F. now gaining an ascendancy in the air, by November 1940 a sufficient mastery of the air force Enigma had also been achieved, which then revealed the enemy's forthcoming policy of launching large scale night attacks on industrial areas, the prelude to the 'Blitz'.

As for the naval Enigma, this initially proved difficult to break, but from U boat U33, in February 1940, Enigma wheels had been captured, and an operation was then mounted to seize a complete machine and its settings. This was accomplished with the capture of the armed trawler 'Krebs', but the code was in the Home Key and the Foreign Key remained elusive. However, the information revealed that German weather ships carried the full naval Enigma machine and the subsequent seizure of the 'München' on May 7th 1941, plus papers seized from the 'Lauenburg', maintained the code breaking ability. The capture of U110, with the cipher equipment intact, then proved invaluable, though the introduction by the Germans of later refinements negated the ability. Compounded by the fact that for a while the Germans were able to read the convoy code, shipping losses had now reached crisis point, but on October 30th 1942 the disabling of U559 provided, through the bravery of two British crew members, not only a modified Enigma but documents as well. Allied with other measures, this now meant that in the Battle of the Atlantic the tide had truly turned, and, unaware of the codebreaking achievements, the Germans assumed that a spy ring was operating at the U boat bases!

However, at Bletchley Park there were also always security concerns, such as one Wednesday at the end of August 1942 when an unknown man, wearing a navy-blue suit, on being challenged about his ticket by the Bletchley station ticket collector, Mr. Roff, had suddenly slipped away and dodging between travellers and railwaymen scaled the wall surrounding Bletchley Park. Despite the police being immediately called, no trace could be found of him. Also mystifying, at least to the Council, was the need under the Defence Regulations to in June 1943 divert and 'stop up' a footpath in Bletchley Park leading to Denbigh Road. It seemed somewhat unusual that a footpath diversion had been submitted to the Quarter Sessions for approval, and the Council thought they 'should know more about the matter'.

With the approach of D Day, the need became increasingly important to break the highly sophisticated cypher – even more so than Enigma – that was used to communicate between Hitler and his generals. Known as Lorenz, initial methods had been by hand but, since this was obviously a slow process, the decoded information would invariably be out of date. Therefore to accomplish the task a machine was constructed appropriately named Robinson, after Heath Robinson, renowned for his cartoon contraptions. From Robinson then evolved a faster electronic machine using valves, and the result would be Colossus, the first programmable electronic computer in the world. This proved of incalculable value in the success of D Day, for not only would it provide the German order of battle, but also reveal the German reaction to the various deceptions that were being employed.

Nevertheless, at the end of the war most of the highly secret and technologically advanced equipment employed at Bletchley Park was disposed of, and, with the staff disbanded, in January 1946 it was announced that Bletchley Park would become the headquarters of the Allied Control Commission, with the first contingent of officials to arrive from their present accommodation at the Grand Hotel, Eastbourne, by the last week of February. They would be housed in hostels on the estate whilst, as for the Park's previous occupants, in April 1946 the head of 'the large and extremely important Government organisation' which had been at Bletchley Park throughout the war wrote to the local Council, stating that; 'The organisation which has been under my charge at Bletchley during the war is now moving to another place and I should like to take the opportunity through you, of thanking all those people in your area who have rendered us so much help and assistance'. 'We have been only to well aware that the billeting of large numbers of people for so long a period has been extremely irksome, and we are most grateful to all those who, uncomplainingly, have put with those impositions'.

APPENDIX B

WOBURN ABBEY – A BRIEF HISTORY

Woburn Abbey played an important role in the wartime intelligence activities of World War Two, yet this was just one phase in a long and colourful past, briefly summarised herewith.

In 1145 Hugh de Bolebec founded a Cistercian abbey at Woburn. In that year fourteen monks came from Fountains Abbey to begin the community, but this did not flourish and by 1234 had become so poor that it was disbanded until the debts were paid off. Yet the abbey remained and from the original village a town developed, granted a yearly fair and a weekly market.

With Henry VIII's declaration as Supreme Head of the English Church, at the Dissolution the fate of the Abbey was sealed, and when Henry's commissioners came to Woburn they found twelve monks, the abbot and the sub prior. Eleven monks were freed but the other three were tried, found guilty and hanged from a tree at the entrance to the priory. Now known as Abbot's Oak, the tree still remains, some two hundred yards from the west front of the building and supposedly the ghost of the Abbot in a long brown robe, is said to haunt the Abbey. Sightings in the crypt and the Sculpture Gallery have been reported.

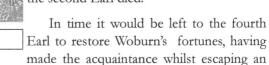

1st Earl of Bedford (Duke of Bedford)

After the Dissolution the interests of the Abbey were granted – by royal award – to a Dorset squire, John Russell, who was eventually created Earl of Bedford in 1550. By marriage, he preferred to live at Chenies, in Buckinghamshire, and so the second Earl was thrown into a state of near panic when, in 1572, the neglected property at Woburn received a visit from Queen Elizabeth. After this regal arrival the Abbey again lay forgotten and in 1585, burdened by debt, the second Earl died.

In time it would be left to the fourth Earl to restore Woburn's fortunes, having made the acquaintance whilst escaping an epidemic of smallpox in London. Apart from various restorations he also made plans to construct a ninety room mansion, the largest in the county. Unfortunately he died from smallpox in 1641 and during those days of the Civil War his son, the 5th Earl, pledged allegiance to the Parliamentary cause. However, growing weary of war, following the failure of peace proposals he then reversed his loyalties, but, having joined the Royalists, became dissatisfied with the King's policy and surrendered to the Earl of Essex in December 1643. His goods at Bedford House were confiscated by Parliament, although he was allowed to remain quietly at Woburn. On May 11th 1694, he was created Duke of Bedford by William and Mary. By marriage his son acquired much property in London, and both Russell Square and Bedford Row are two continuing reminders.

4th Duke of Bedford (Duke of Bedford)

Eventually it was the fourth Duke of Bedford, John, who began the rebuilding of Woburn Abbey. Much had to be demolished, but nevertheless the resulting reconstructions preserved the quadrangular plan. His grandson became the 5th Duke and although not given to a scholarly disposition was nevertheless fond of home entertainments, installing his mistress in a wing of the Abbey! Yet he commissioned the famed Henry Holland to add the east front of the Abbey and also, in the form of a broad, sweeping semi circle, the main entrance to the Park. His brother, John, inherited the estate in 1802 and engaged Humphrey Repton to lay out a suitably impressive approach to the west front.

11th Duke of Bedford (Duke of Bedford)

John's third son, also John, twice became Prime Minister but it was Francis, the eldest son, who inherited Woburn and a heavy burden of debt, despite which incumberance he still had to provide a 'lavish entertainment' when Queen Victoria and Prince Albert came to visit. The 7th Duke was succeeded in 1861 by his son, William, who built the magnificent church of Woburn between 1865/66 at a cost of £40,000. Somewhat of a recluse, William transferred the management of the estates to his cousin, Francis Charles Hastings. In time he became the 9th Duke but unfortunately later went mad and in 1891 shot himself.

He was succeeded by his eldest son, George, but when he died suddenly, two years later, in the absence of children the inheritance then passed to his brother Herbrand, rather disrespectfully termed 'Hatband' by his fellow associates, when serving in the Grenadier Guards. In time he became the 11th Duke and, not one for modern improvements, he refused to install central heating in the Abbey and instead during the winters relied on nearly eighty wood fires. As for other modern improvements, an early attempt to install electricity came to an abrupt end when a section of the wiring caught fire. At a later attempt, since the Duke would allow no workmen to be seen in his presence, whenever he approached, those laying the cables had to scurry into a cupboard!

In poor health, Herbrand died in 1940 and after the war the Abbey had deteriorated to such a degree that much reconstruction was needed, and in fact the eastern wing had to be demolished. Tragically the 12th Duke died from a gunshot wound whilst out hunting and, although he had made provisions to escape estate duties, he died before these could take effect. As a result his son, the 13th Duke, inherited a tax bill of £4 million, and as for the Abbey, not only had the whole of the east front now gone but also at least a third of the north and south wings. With everywhere in chaos and disorder, by sheer determination the Duke organised a clearing up and renovation, such that in 1955 the Abbey opened to fare-paying visitors, the first arriving in two cars and a bike! In recent years the Safari Park has been but one added attraction and, on the retirement of his parents, the 14th Duke and Duchess of Bedford, the estate came under the management of the Marquess of Tavistock. With his recent sad death, the responsibilities now lie with his son, the present Duke of Bedford.

The present Duke of Bedford

Index

A

A.B.C. 24
Abwehr 128
Acton. Thelma 134
Adam, Ernst 52
Adams, Major 70
Adams, Walter 23
Ainsley, Second Lieutenant 37
Albert, Dr. 98
Albert Hall 96
Anderson, Sir John 64
Andreas, Father 83
Arkley 127
Aspidistra iii, 35, 40, 44, 57, 58, 84, 89, 93, 94, 95, 97, 98, 99, 104
Aspley Guise viii, 21, 47, 49, 51, 52, 53, 54, 56, 57, 66, 67, 71, 81, 83, 85, 88, 99
Aspley Heath 90
Aspley Hill 90
Aston Abbots 90
Aylesbury 126, 137

B

Backhouse, Sir Roger 15
Baker, Captain 135
Barman, Thomas 78
Barry, Mr. 71
Bartlett, Vernon 21
Battlesden 77, 93, 137
B.B.C. 12, 21, 23, 28, 30, 33, 34, 48, 50, 57, 63, 64, 66, 75, 77, 86, 95, 114, 129
Beaverbrook, Lord 33, 47
Belgium 28, 68, 110, 128, 142
Benes, Edvard 12
Bennett, Arnold 13
Bentinck, Rev. Charles Cavendish 77
Berlin 13
Bermuda 13
Bertrand, Colonel 129
Bicester 70
Birmingham 70
Bismarck 70

Bletchley v, viii, 1, 5, 6, 30, 37, 41, 45, 46, 51, 54, 55, 56, 90, 104, 113, 115, 116, 117, 119, 121, 124, 125, 126, 127, 128, 129, 131, 135, 141, 142, 143, 144, 145, 146
Bletchley Park v, viii, 1, 5, 6, 30, 54, 55, 56, 90, 104, 113, 115, 116, 117, 119, 121, 124, 125, 126, 127, 128, 129, 141, 142, 143, 144, 145, 146
Blum, Leon 69
Blunt, Anthony 126
Boscombe Down 134
Boswell, James 9
Bowden, Norman 41
Bowes Lyon, David 19, 32, 33, 73, 75, 77, 84
Bracken, Brendan 65, 73, 74, 76, 78, 86, 99
Braun, Max 52, 96
Broadway 113
Bromley, Ken 117
Bruce Lockhart, Robert 6, 9, 12, 64, 65, 73, 94, 97
Buckingham 35, 45, 46, 138
Bulgaria 68, 97
Burgess, Guy 61
Burney, Colonel Henry 31
Burney, Rev. Henry 31
Bush House 43, 75, 76, 77, 78, 86, 87, 88, 99

C

Cadogan, Sir Alexander 16
Calder, Ritchie 77
Calverton Weald 117, 118
Campbell Stuart, Sir C. 13, 14, 15, 19, 21, 22, 23, 32, 33, 54, 61
Canada 13
Castleman, Captain 121
Cavendish Bentinck 28
Central Ammunition Field Storage) 138
Chamberlain, Neville 17, 25, 143
Chambers, Colonel 85
Chandos Arms, Winslow 135
Chestnut Farm 72
Chicheley Hall 12, 71, 72, 141
Child, Clifton 96
Chittleburgh, William 128
Churchill, Winston 1, 33, 52, 61, 62, 65, 71, 73, 74, 89, 94
Cirencester 1

Cock Hotel, Stony Stratford 1, 33, 52, 61, 62, 65, 71, 73, 74, 89, 94
Colby, Lt. 85
Cole, Colonel 94
Coleman, Russell 'Rusty' 35
College Farm 35
College of Aeronautics 35
Cologne 35
Combined Services Detailed Interrogation Centre 95
Conseil de Resistance 71
Cooper, Duff 33
Coward, Noel 19
Cowgill, Felix 128
Cox, Staff Sergeant 41
Cranfield 87, 120, 133, 134
Crewe House 13, 15
Cripps, Stafford 51
Crossman, Richard 50, 51, 66, 67
Crowborough 90
Curtis, Canon 114
Czechoslovakia 12, 15
Czechoslovak Secret Intelligence 12

D

Daily Express 47, 48, 81
Dallas Brooks, Lt. Col (later Major General) 11, 15, 19, 23, 33, 63, 64, 65, 73, 75, 86
Dalton, Hugh 33, 62, 63, 64, 65, 67, 69, 73, 74, 89, 96
d'Auvert, Louisa 52
Dawn Edge', Aspley Guise, 67
D Day 44, 85, 86, 99, 102, 107, 110, 126, 131, 142, 145
Delmer, Sefton iii, v, viii, 47, 48, 49, 50, 51, 52, 53, 54, 55, 56, 57, 69, 71, 72, 79, 81, 83, 84, 85, 86, 88, 89, 94, 95, 97, 98, 99, 102, 104, 107, 110
Department Electra House iii, 1, 9, 15, 18, 19, 20, 21, 23, 28, 30, 32, 33, 34, 61, 62, 65, 66, 77, 79, 80, 112
Der Londoner Brief 28
Deutscher Kurzwellen-sender Atlantik 55
Deutsches Nachrichtenburo 51
Dietrich, Marlene 96
Diplomatic Wireless Service 126, 130
Dorchester Hotel 87, 88

Dougherty, Jim 50
Drayton Parslow 72
Duchess of Bedford, Mary 1, 11, 21, 25, 29, 56, 90, 133, 149
Duggan, Patsy' 124
Duke of Bedford v, 8, 19, 20, 21, 53, 62, 68, 90, 105, 133, 147, 148, 149
Dunkley, Walter 123
Dunstable 10, 19, 25, 91

E

Eagles Nest 103
Eden, Anthony 11, 14, 64, 65, 73, 74, 78, 83, 89
Elias, General 12
Elliot, John 107
European Revolution Station 66

F

Fenny Stratford repeater station 5, 6, 141
Fernet, Admiral 21
Field, Gracie 98
Fisher, Sir Warren 15
Fisher, Tommy 120
Fitzmaurice Place 11, 73, 75
Fitzpatrick, Captain Molly 57
Fleming, Ian 56
Florent, Capitaine 'Perfi' 82
Foxgrove, Woburn Abbey 9
France 12, 17, 21, 22, 32, 33, 54, 61, 65, 68, 69, 82, 110, 112, 128, 134, 143
Fritzsche, Hans 51
Fuller, Hal 37

G

Gaitskell, Hugh 62, 63, 64, 96
Gambier Parry, Brig. Sir Richard 30, 32, 36, 38, 68, 84, 89, 90, 91, 95, 113, 114, 126, 128, 129
Gardenia 36, 37, 40
Gawcott 31, 35, 36, 37, 39, 40, 41, 55, 68, 89, 93, 129, 141
Geranium 36, 37, 40
Gibson, Guy 134
Gillie, Darsie 66
Gishford, Anthony 19
Glendining, Dr. 56

Goebbels, Josef 26, 55, 58, 87
Gort, Lord 129
G (R) 61
Grange Farm, Milton Bryan 91
Grendon Underwood 70, 141
Groves, Air Commodore 28
Guardian, Manchester 54
Gubbins, Colonel Colin 69
Gustav Seigfried Eins 69
Gutmann, Hans 98

H

Hackett, Major John 85
Haffner, Dr. 68
Halifax, Lord 14, 15
Halkett, Renee 54
Halliday, Edward, Squadron Leader v, 35, 54, 59, 83, 90, 91, 92, 94, 95, 97, 100
Hanslope Park 5, 104, 113, 114, 128, 129, 130, 141
Harman, Terry 32
Hatch Manson wine merchants 127
Hawker Typhoon 131
Heatley, Bill 37
Hellschreiber 41, 52, 83, 110
Hess, Rudolf 24, 50
Heydrich, Reinhard 12
Hillman Minx 38
Himmler 48, 96, 103, 104
Hockliffe 6, 12, 13, 77
Hodgkin, Squadron Leader 110
Hodson, Miss 85
Holden, Ewart 117
Holland 61, 110, 128, 148
Holland, Colonel J. 61
Holland, Henry 148
Home Guard 37, 68, 129
Honneur et Patrie 71
Hoover Library. 13
Horsa glider 131

I

Imperial Communications Advisory Board 24, 33
Inglis, Sir Robert 93
Ingrams, Leonard 33, 49, 52, 79
Isle of Man 66

Italy 25, 68, 97

J

John O'Groats 127
John, Otto 102
Johnson, Dr. 9
Joint Intelligence Committee 71
Jones, Percy 41

K

Keeble, Harold 78, 79, 81, 107
Keen, Major Dick 128
King George VI and Queen Elizabeth 76
King-Hall, Commander 65
Kingsbury, Mr. 67
Kirkpatrick, Ivone 75, 86

L

La France Catholique 82
Lagrave, Capitaine 82
Land's End 127
Lansdowne House 11, 63
Latimer 93
Lawson, Mr 91
Leagrave Press 107
Leamington Spa 12
Leatherhead 128
Le Courier de L'Air 81
Leeper, Reginald 9, 10, 11, 12, 33, 48, 52, 62, 63, 65, 66, 67, 73, 76, 78, 97
Libya 81
Limb, Wilfred 128
Lisbon 48, 51, 102
Little Brickhill 77
Little Horwood 46, 113, 120, 121, 122, 123, 124, 125, 126, 135, 136, 142
Locarno Pact 74
Locarno Room, Foreign Office 74
London 74, 113
London Recording Unit 74
Lord Haw Haw 54
L'Orient 135
Lothar, Dr 68
Louisa d'Auvert 52
Lowndes Arms 116
Luck, Phil 37
Luton, Alma Street 107

Luton News 24, 107, 110, 111, 112
Lynder, Frank 54
Lyons and Co., J 24
Lysander, Westland 70

M

Maas, Alexander 52, 54
Madagascar 85
Maddy, Freda 52
Magnetofon 31
Malta 114
Maltby, Colonel Edward 128, 129
Manchester 96
Marler, Major I 31
Martelli, George 9
Martin Baker MB3 135
Marylands, nr. Woburn v, 10, 11, 25, 29, 76,
      78, 85, 107, 110, 133
Maude, Mrs C. 72
McLachlan, Lt. Commander 56, 110
McMillan, Lord 15
Meikle, Mr 78
Menzies 113
Menzies, Colonel Stuart 113
Metherell, Lt. Colonel 78
Mexico 98
Miller, Glenn 134
Milton Bryan iii, v, 1, 38, 40, 57, 58, 59, 69,
      78, 81, 83, 84, 85, 89, 91, 92, 93, 94,
      95, 96, 97, 98, 99, 100, 104, 105, 107,
      110
Milton Keynes, Abbots Close 114
Ministry of Information 76
MI (R) 61, 62, 69
Montgomery, Field Marshall 129
Moravia 12
Morgan, John 134
Morrison, Squadron Leader 112
Morton, Jack 41
Moscow 9
Mosquito, de Havilland 134
Munich 9, 15, 143
Munroe bomb 110
Munroe, Capt. James 112
Murray, Ingram v, 105
Murray, Sir Ralph 32, 34, 71, 90
Mursley 135

N

Nachrichten für die Truppe 81, 99, 107
Nash 117, 126
near Barnet 127
Nelson, Frank 69
New Inn, Gawcott 37
Newport Pagnell 14, 19, 72, 115
New York 14, 62, 65
North Africa 44
Northampton 115
Northcliffe, Lord 14
North Crawley 9
Norway 110, 128
Notre Dame Cathedral, Paris 81

O

Occult Station (G6) 83
O'Connor, Jack 41
Old Rectory, Woburn 62
Operation Torch 85
Oundle 30, 35
Oxford, Airspeed 135
Oxford, Balliol College 13
Oxford, Lincoln College 47
Oxford University Press 25

P

Packard 126
Paddington, London 116
Pansy 42, 43, 44, 45
Paris 142, 143
Paris Exhibition, 1878 90
Paris House 21, 23, 90, 91
Peake Clothing Factory, Bletchley 131
Pearl Harbour 78
Pertenhall 85
Philby, Kim 63
Philco 30, 35, 113, 114, 128
Phillips, Major 70
P.I.D. 9, 10, 11, 12, 13, 38, 73, 76
Pidgeon, Horace 117
Place de la Concorde 21
Poland 21
Polish agents 72
Pollard, Alex 117
Poole, Dorset 102
Poppy 43, 44, 45

Portugal 28
Potsgrove 35, 37, 38, 41, 42, 43, 44, 45, 55, 68, 89, 90, 93, 129, 141
Poundon 70, 141
Prague 25
Prickett, Captain 129
Prickett, Jim 37
Pryke, Thomas 35, 37
P.W.E. 38, 70, 73, 74, 75, 76, 77, 78, 79, 80, 81, 82, 84, 85, 86, 87, 88, 95, 97, 99, 107
Pytchley Hunt 77

R

Radio Inconnue 67
Radio Patrie 70
RADIO SECURITY SERVICE 126
Radio Travail 67
Radlett, Herts 86
R.A.F. 26 O.T.U. 137
R.A.F. 138 Squadron 70
R.A.F. Groups 28, 40, 41, 64, 70, 71, 81, 95, 98, 110, 112, 115, 116, 132, 134, 144, 145
Ramshaw, Mrs 129
Rastenburg, East Prussia 102
R.C.A. 36, 66, 89
Reeday, George 113
Reichstag 48
Reinholz, Johannes 50
Research Units 66, 68
Ridgmont, Beds. 77, 133
Ritson, Mrs 107
Robin, Harold 30, 31, 32, 35, 38, 43, 44, 65, 83, 84, 89, 90, 93, 94, 95, 98, 104
Robson, Major Karl 95
'Rockex' system 129
Romania 97
Rookery, The 52, 53, 57, 71, 81, 84, 85, 88, 102
Roosevelt, President F D 73, 95
Rose Cottages, Winslow 135
Ross, Sir John 12
Royal Corps of Signals 117
Royal Flying Corps 114
Royal Welch Fusiliers 114
Rushton Hornsby 37
Russell, The Hon. Leo 19

Russia 9, 26, 52, 53, 141

S

Sachs, Brig. Eric 78
Saint Vincent's school 21
Samuel, Mrs 62
Sargent, Sir Orme 11
Savoy Hotel, London 86
Scott, L/Corporal Lily 45
Scout Association 104
SCU1 113, 120, 122
SCU3 113, 130
Seckelmann, Peter 49, 51
Section D 61, 62, 69
Sedgwick, Lt. Col. 85
Shaw, R.J. 15
Sheldon, Ralph (Lord Sandhurst) 127
Shenley Brook End 129
Shenley Church End 113
Sheridan, Capt. 71
Sherwood, Robert E. 73
Shildon, Durham 74
Sikorski, General 81
Sinclair, Admiral Sir Hugh 15, 113, 128, 143
Skorpion West 81
Smith, Alan 123
Smith, Michael Gibbs 19
Smith, Mrs D 114
Smith, William 14
S.O.E. 1, 12, 33, 55, 57, 61, 62, 63, 69, 70, 72, 81, 85, 104
Soldatensender Calais 40, 44, 55, 57, 58, 97, 104
South Africa 15
Spain 28
Spanish Civil War 52, 98
Special Leaflet Squadron 110
Special Liaison Units 121, 142
Special Training School 71, 72
S phone 120
Spiecker, Dr. Klaus 32
Steadman, Sergeant 45
Steinbeck, John 71
Stephens, David 73
St. Ermins hotel 61
Stevens, C. 96
Stewart Roberts, Mrs 23
Stirling, Short 132, 133

Stockholm 28
Stony Stratford 120
Strang, William 11
Strathmore, Lady 77
Streatham 8
Stuchly, Lt. Jaroslav 12
Sun Engraving Co. 25
Sussex 90
Sweden 55
Switzerland 28
Swordfish, Fairey 137

T

Tattenhoe Bare 114, 115, 116, 119
TATTENHOE CAMP 45
Taylor, Clifford 118
Taylor, Rebekah 118
Tempsford, Beds. 12, 69, 70
Thame Park, Bucks. 70
The Anchor, Aspley Guise 67
'The Firs', Whitchurch 71
The Holt, Aspley Guise 99
The Lodge, Bullington End, Hanslope 128
The Mount, Aspley Guise 82
Thetford, Norfolk 93
Thomas Bates Company 91
Thomas Cook and Son 24
Toddington, Beds. 67
Todd-Thornton, Mrs 78
Tonschreiber 31
Towse, Lisa 30, 114
Tree, Ronald 76
Turing, Alan 104, 129
Turner, Edward 121
Turney, Jack 44
Tweedie, Mr 47
Twickenham 117
Twinwoods Farm 134
Tyler, Tim 78

U

U.S.A.A.F., 91st Bombardment Group 135
U.S.A.A.F., 305th Group 110
U.S.A.A.F., 422nd Squadron 110

V

V1 75, 86, 87, 95, 134

V2 87
Vienna 25
Voight, Freddy 54
Voluntary Interceptors 127, 128
Von Thoma, General 55

W

Walton Rectory 90
Warner, Chris 9
Warr, William 52
Warsaw 47
Washington 84
Waterlows, Dunstable 25
Watford 28
Watts, Arthur 127
Wavendon Towers 31, 32, 35, 38, 41, 50, 55,
        65, 67, 68, 76, 77, 85, 91, 95, 113
Weatherhead, Bert 41
Weimar Republic 32
Wellington bombers 135
West, Charles 121
Whaddon 1, 30, 31, 32, 34, 35, 65, 113, 114,
        115, 116, 117, 118, 119, 120, 121, 122,
        126, 128, 130, 142
Whaddon Chase 115
Whaddon church 113, 115, 119
Whaddon Main Line 113
Whipsnade Zoo 70
Whitchurch 71
Whitehall 43, 62, 113, 144
White House, Washington 95
White, Major 28
Whitley, Armstrong Whitworth 126, 131,
        132
W.I.C.O.s Electrical Company 131
Wigg, Reginald 129
Williamson, Cecil 31, 65
Williams, Valentine 11, 15, 28, 33, 48, 62, 65
Willis, Commander 94
Wilsher, Andy 112
Wilson, Mr 91
Wilton Park. 93
Windy Ridge 113, 115, 116, 119, 126
Wing 133, 135, 137
Wing House 85
Wingrave 12
Winslow 6, 12, 135
WJ2 New Jersey 89

Woburn, 6, Leighton Street 63
Woburn Abbey viii, 1, 9, 15, 19, 20, 21, 23,
          25, 52, 53, 64, 75, 78, 81, 87, 89, 90,
          93, 97, 132, 133, 141, 147, 148
Woburn Park 9, 21, 24, 91
Woldingham, Surrey 12
Wolkiger Beobachter 25
Wolverton Works, Wolverton 131
Woodcote, Aspley Guise 56
Woodward, E. 9
Worlledge, Major J. 127
Wormwood Scrubs 127

Z

Zeisel, Henry 96

Books by John A. Taylor

Bletchley Histories

Bletchley Park's Secret Sisters.
Bletchley Town Historical Trail.
Bletchley and District at War.
Bletchley Buckinghamshire. The Railway Story.

Local Histories

Ampthill, Bedfordshire. (A short history).
Flitwick, Bedfordshire. (A short history).
Broughton, Buckinghamshire. (A short history).
Swanbourne, Buckinghamshire. (A short history).
Milton Keynes. An Aeronautical Past.
Newton Longville. A Glance at Times Gone By.
The Aspley Guise and Woburn Sands Gas Works:The Early Years.
Tale of Two Cities: A history of the Milton Keynes district before the New City. *(Published as a series of 25 articles by the Milton Keynes Mirror; May 9th - Oct. 24th 1979).*
City Limits. (Town & village histories, within 12 miles of Milton Keynes).

About the First World War

Stony Stratford during the First World War
Newport Pagnell during the First World War
Home Fires: Life in the North Bucks Towns and Villages during the First World War
Bletchley During the First World War.
Wolverton during the First World War: Volume 1
Wolverton during the First World War: Volume 2
Urgent Copy: Reports from the Wolverton Express about the First World War (with Bryan Dunleavy)
Voices from the First World War. (Letters from the archives of the North Bucks Times.)

Lightning Source UK Ltd.
Milton Keynes UK
UKHW032030220321
380796UK00006B/126